Age **60** to **120**
Live it Up
in the
New Millennium

Vitality

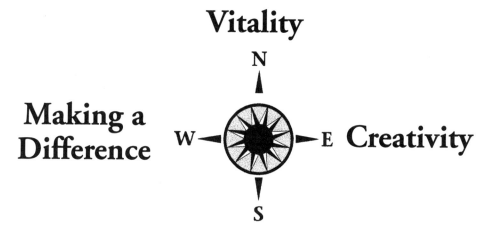

Making a Difference

Creativity

Fun Function

Proctor Publications, LLC

Proctor Publications
P.O. Box 2498
Ann Arbor, Michigan 48106
(800) 343-3034

Printed in the United States of America

Publisher's Cataloging-in-Publication
(Provided by Quality Books, Inc.)

Plummer, Robert H.
    Age 60 to 120 : live it up in the new
millennium / [Bob Plummer]. -- 1st ed.
        p. cm.
    LCCN: 99-75132
    ISBN: 1-882792-88-2

    1. Aging. 2. Longevity--Popular works.
3. Aging--Prevention--Popular works. 4. Age factors
in disease--Popular works. 5. Aged--Diseases--
Popular works. 6. Aged--Health and hygiene--
Popular works. I. Title

QP86.P68 1999 2000   612.67
                                QBI99-500556

TABLE OF CONTENTS

- Introduction ....*iv*

- Vitality
  Winning the War Against the Enemies.................. 1

- Creativity 56

- Fun Function — Renewal 91

- Making a Difference 155

- Living It Up Daily Reminders 178

- Useful Related Sources 179

- About the Author .... *vii*

As time advances
vitality, activity, laughter,
and love strengthen us,
creating exultation.

Bob Plummer

INTRODUCTION

Can length of life be extended? In 1900 life expectancy was 47 years. At the end of the century, the year 2000, 16 million Americans are in their late seventies. This figure will probably almost double to 30 million in another 50 years. Is it possible that science can add another 40 years of relatively good health? The Journal of Science reports that Geron scientists at Texas Southwestern University Medical Center have shown that telemeres (the ends of cells), which divide 50 times to allow around 100 years of life, can be added to for twenty more divisions for possibly another 40 years of life. They think that degenerative diseases may be treated with these renewed cells. The New York Times of March 9, 1999 reported a lecture that Dr. Campiri, at the University of California-Berkeley, gave on this possibility.

In these later years there may be reduced hearing, impotence, a few tremors, some back pain. We can always be renewed by activity. Retired admirals paint houses, others have garden plots, and many find volunteer activities that abound in every community.

At the beginning of the new millennium there are over 60,000 persons in the United States over the age of 100; these numbers are growing rapidly. At age 110, Milton Garland, of Waynesboro, Pennsylvania, was working 20 hours a week as a part time engineer. The oldest documented person at this writing is Jeanne Louise Calment of France, who died in 1997 at the age of 122 years. A stellar example of continuing vitality is never-married Emma Buck, at age 95 walking around her 80 acre farm, which has no plumbing, in Monroe County, Illinois, fetching water with a wooden bucket from a well house and sharpening her scythe on a foot-operated grinding wheel in the threshing shed.

Robert Browning's admonition was, "Grow old along with me! The best is yet to be; the last for which the first was made." John Glenn returned to space at age 77 after serving in the U.S. Senate for over twenty years. People over that age are climbing mountains. President Jimmy Carter has written thirteen books since retiring, runs marathons, and takes goodwill trips worldwide.

Moving into a new century we are all challenged to use advanced information for increasing our vitality. Information is expected to double every ten years. Computers now hook together all known and developing information. Putting value into longer life is a frontier as challenging as the Western frontier was to our ancestors. Ferdinand Magellan sailed west in 1521 to discover the Philippines. Robert Perry was the first to reach the North Pole in 1909. Ronald Amundsen was the first to reach the South Pole in 1911. Charles Lindbergh was the first to unite two continents by air by flying east in 1927.

A new frontier beckons. Time is available for us to box the compass in four directions toward vitality, creativity, fun function, and making a difference. As age 20 plans ahead toward 40, age 40 toward 60, age 60 toward 80, the newest frontier is for age 80 to plan toward 100+. Psychologist Karen Horney says we have the capacity to change and grow as long as we live, keeping young and contemporary. Satchel Paige, longtime all-American baseball player, when asked about his age, replied, "How old would you be if you didn't know how old you is?"

The author, at age 85, is planning toward age 100+ and welcomes all aboard for a good sail to what is, for the first time in history, a reasonable goal in the 21st century.

Chapter One

Vitality — Winning the War Against the Enemies

"When you are young you challenge your body. Now your body challenges you."
M. Baryshnikov, Dancer and Choreographer

Enemy Number One: Heart Disease or Stroke

Enemy Number Two: Cancer

Enemy Number Three: Alzheimer's Disease

Enemy Number Four: Influenza and Colds

Other Enemies: Arthritis, Osteoporosis, Parkinson's Disease

Overlooked One-third of Life: Sleep Renewal

Hearing and Vision in Aging

Beating Stress and Depression: Laugh and Be Healthy

Road Rage and Safety

Looking to the Future

ENEMY NUMBER ONE: HEART DISEASE OR STROKE

Half a million Americans die each year from heart disease or stroke. With dizziness and chest pain, first call 911 for an ambulance and take an aspirin. The nearest hospital may not be the best. Hospitals with the highest volume of heart treatment are most likely to save your life. But help within three hours is critical. Automatic emergency heart defibrillators can give an immediate life-saving shock in an emergency. Such equipment is available in stadiums, office buildings, even casinos.

In the near future mechanical devices may eliminate the need for human heart transplants, becoming routine as the 20th century ends. On the horizon are implanted ventricular assistance devices, "IVADs". They allow great mobility since the power source, a battery pack, can be carried in a waist belt.

A healthy heart is a marvelous life-renewing pump the size of a fist and weighing less than a pound. It can pump 24 hours a day for well over 100 years sending renewed fresh blood through miles of the circulatory system. Yet a Harvard Medical School study reports that 25 extra pounds can result in a 2 1/2 greater chance of heart failure. Half of all Americans are overweight — 300,000 die each year as a result of obesity.

If we take the following government's weight table seriously, the permitted ranges may seem like the wide-open spaces. We do have to make some allowance for our bone structure and gender. Though this single table covers all people, women tend to have less muscle and smaller bones than men the same size, so they should stick to the lower end of the ranges, while large-boned men will need to aim at the higher end. These weights are without clothes or shoes.

HEIGHT	WEIGHT
4'10"	91-119
4'11"	94-124
5'0"	97-128
5'1"	101-132
5'2"	104-137
5'3"	107-141
5'4"	111-146
5'5"	114-150
5'6"	118-155
5'7"	121-160
5'8"	125-164
5'9"	129-169
5'10"	132-174
5'11"	136-179
6'0"	140-184
6'1"	144-189
6'2"	148-195
6'3"	152-200
6'4"	156-205
6'5"	160-211
6'6"	164-216

At the beginning of the century just passed, life expectancy was in the mid-forties, by the end of the century in the mid-seventies. In the new millennium an equal gain can bring it to the

100-year average. Self-discipline in calorie intake and increased oxygen intake from exercise will renew the heart and blood vessels, reduce stiffening of the joints, and aid in extending life.

Americans get most of their complex carbohydrates from refined grains that are stripped of their fiber and many nutrients. Sugars and refined starches offer little to no nutrition except calories and possible disease. More whole grains are the answer to strengthen the heart and circulation. If the content reads, "enriched wheat or wheat flour", it is a refined product. To reverse aging 30 to 40 years, scientists recommend free radicals from fruits and vegetables full of vitamins C and E and adding exercise to the formula.

Thieves to health are French fries, whole milk, most varieties of cheese, many dressings, and red meat. On the positive side are commonly available meat-free veggie burgers. A growing number of Americans are discovering soybeans aren't just for livestock, but soybean products lower heart disease, fight cancer, and build healthy bones.

One early study showed that Bantu Africans get 25 grams of fibrous food daily: grains, vegetables, seeds, yogurt, and potatoes; while English schoolboys got only three grams of fibrous food on a diet of highly processed foods. The school boys kept food in their bodies for up to 36 hours compared to 12 hours for the Africans. The incidence of colon cancer was three times greater for the English schoolboys. The longer the colon containment, the shorter the life span.

The Food Guide Pyramid recommends a variety of carbohydrates from the following food groups:

6 to 9 servings of grains

3 to 4 servings of vegetables

2 to 3 servings of fruits

2 to 3 servings of dairy products

Richly colored fruits are recommended — green, orange, red, or yellow. Vegetables such as broccoli, cauliflower, kale, and mustard greens are rich in disease-blocking chemicals. Good sources for calcium are low fat milk, fortified orange juice, yogurt, and hard cheese. The superstar nutrient is calcium, contributing to nearly every organ system. It is the most abundant mineral in the body, maintaining strong bones and teeth.

One bit of good news for chocolate lovers is that chemicals in chocolate may reduce the plaque in blocked arteries. Also, chemicals in wine have been linked to a lower risk of heart disease and stroke. It is important to limit oneself to one or two drinks a day, however. Red wine is especially beneficial.

Hippocrates declared 2,500 years ago, "Let food be your medicine and medicine be your food."

Reduced thirst is a characteristic of aging, but the general recommendation for water is eight 8-ounce glasses daily to maintain blood pressure and kidney function. A free treatment every waking hour is to replenish the body with a small glass of room temperature water.

Dr. Everett Koop, former Surgeon General of the United States, says that the lack of activity in the population is at crisis proportions and that activity is essential to reducing premature death. He reports that 60% of Americans are not active on a regular basis and 25% are not active at all. We can walk almost anywhere anytime finding a nearby path void of vehicle exhaust. Walking can be done in any weather with proper gear, except in heavy rain or snow when we can move indoors to halls or malls. Ideal is a minimum of a mile of vigorous stride six days a week with Sunday off. If necessary for safety and / or support, we can use a cane or a walker. The pluses are sevenfold:

1. Greater energy and endurance from oxygen utilization
2. Improved weight control and body tone
3. Greater ability to prevent or handle accidents
4. A euphoric feeling due to release of endorphins
5. Slowing the aging process with better sleep
6. Improved thinking capacity and productivity
7. Renewal from the trees we pass under, the flora we see, and the fresh air carrying pure oxygen to the lungs

Only one out of four Americans exercises daily. Three out of four gain weight as they age. Walking a minimum of a mile every day not only strengthens the heart but also reduces breast cancer in women by one-third. Walking exercise backs up the clock keeping the mind young for both men and women.

Exercise can also be done lying in bed on our back before rising by pumping the legs to simulate riding a bicycle, even concurrently boxing the air with the fists. Still in bed we can do leg lifts, ankle twists, knee pulls, and rises of the buttocks. Sitting on the edge of the bed, we can do leg lifts, leg crosses, and bending to touch the floor. Standing in our four by four-foot "gym", we can skip rope without a rope to avoid danger.

With inexpensive equipment, such as a bungee (elastic) rope, available in medical supply stores in packages at about 70 cents a foot, and knotted at each end, we can exercise our arms and shoulders. The length needed is equal to one half the extent of one's outstretched arms. We can stretch our arms out in front, overhead, and behind the back. Sitting on the side of a bed or on a chair, we can place the bungee rope under the feet and then pull to create a rowing machine.

With minimum expense to create a running track in our bedroom gym, we can get a new or used yell leader's small trampoline and shorten its legs to slide under the bed for storage. By running in place on the trampoline, preferably concurrently swinging two-pound weights, we have found an easy way of running. Internal lymph glands are exercised by jumping up and down.

If indoors and stairs are not available, we can mock climbing by using a low kitchen stool while holding a cane or broomstick for safety.

We can do these exercises at age 90+ with two-pound weights or soup cans, or half-gallon plastic milk cartons filled with water. Filling a carton with sand makes a four-pound weight. The illustration on the next page is good example.

A woman in her 90's ran a mile in 13 minutes. Herb Kink of Beaverton, Oregon, at age 101, ran two miles in 36 minutes. If overweight, anyone can lose 10 pounds with diet and exercise, significantly preserving health.

Morbidity is less in women partly due to their carrying excess weight around the hips, while men carry excess weight around the waist crowding the vital organs of heart, liver, and lungs.

Here are stretching exercises to keep active:

Exercise 1

Exercise 2

Exercise3

Exercise 4

Exercise5

Another factor in heart disease is the amount of smoking by either sex. The American Lung Association reports that 70% of smokers have tried to stop smoking but failed. Quitting "cold turkey" is the most difficult. There are aids on the market, such as nicotine gum and hollow inhalers. When a person ceases to smoke, the heart and lungs return to normal within five years.

With a home device we can monitor blood pressure to get two readings — diastolic and systolic. The goal is no higher than 140/90. It is best to measure blood pressure both sitting and standing. The difference between the two readings is best if 45-50, not 75.

Subject of a 1999 public television program was a three hour review of the book by Fred Warshopsky entitled *Stealing Time: The New Science of Aging*, which is an excellent read.

An example of anti-aging in the United States is Sara Knauss at age 118 pictured in The New York Times with her great-great-great grandson, age five. They both have winning smiles. Another example is U.S. Senator Strom Thurmond, at age 96, an influential politician from South Carolina. His secret has been a diet and exercise program along with good family support. Who will be the first in the U.S. to pass age 120? The French have done it, Vive la France; but Americans can too.

A stroke, a brain attack, is similar to a heart attack. Blood vessels in the brain either burst or more commonly become blocked. Severe strokes can be fatal; others can impair speech, vision, movement, or even cause paralysis and coma. By dissolving clots, a drug called TPA, brand name *Activase*, may restore blood flow but only if used within three hours of the attack. In clinical trials other drugs are coming online to protect remaining live cells from the destructive chemicals released by dying cells. According to recent studies, smokers are twice as likely as nonsmokers to have a stroke.

One technique for resting the heart while sitting at rest is to cross the arms over the chest and cross the legs. The heart doesn't have to pump blood so far and in returning to the right side of the heart, blood is pumped into the lungs to absorb oxygen. An added relaxing diversion is solo dancing. Anyone who can walk can do the "two step" with a humming or singing accompaniment.

One up-to-date source of information on health and fitness is now presented weekly in The New York Times; each Tuesday is a section called "Science Times". One may find reported there that marriage, or remarriage if widowed, benefits both men and women, boosting physical and emotional health and raising income.

Monthly Health Letters found in hospital and public libraries or available by subscription:
Harvard Health Letter
Johns Hopkins Health Letter
    (Compilation in *Johns Hopkins Family Health Book*, 1999)
Mayo Clinic Health Letter
Tufts University Health and Nutrition Letter
University of California, Berkeley Health Letter

In many libraries are popular magazines on health:
American Health
Consumers Reports

Geriatrics

Health

Modern Maturity

New Choices

Nutrition Today

ENEMY NUMBER TWO: CANCER

Cancer kills 1,500 Americans each day, over 650,000 in a recent year. One out of four men dies of cancer. Avoidance hinges on the same preventatives as for heart disease and stroke: daily exercise, a good diet, limited alcohol, and not smoking.

If we realize the relationship of smoking to lung cancer, the idea of a smoke-free society becomes intriguing. Nagging or preaching to smokers does not work. Scientists have learned of the trickery by which nicotine is able to work itself into the cells of the brain producing, among other things, dopamine and norepinephrine, the first contributing to a feeling of joy and pleasure, the latter increasing energy and concentration. The problem is that nicotine causes rapid surges and then rapid depletion of these chemicals, leaving the smoker yearning for another cigarette.

Smoking causes cancers in the lungs, in the mouth, in the throat, the pancreas, the bladder, the kidneys, and the colon. It is estimated that tobacco costs over $2.00 in medical expenses for every cigarette smoked and kills thousands of people each year in the United States. Cancer of the lung is estimated to be 1,000 % higher in smokers than in those who never smoke, as well as being a leading cause of heart disease. Health experts link smoking with sexual dysfunction. In addition, those who smoke develop shriveled skin and wrinkles. Yet in spite of these studies and results, 40% of Americans still smoke. Some take it as a sign of sophistication. Cigars are almost as lethal as cigarettes. The benefits of stopping are immediate. In five years a person's health may return to what it was before smoking.

Passive exposure to tobacco smoke is a public health issue for everyone. <u>The New York Times</u> has led the way by banning ciga-rette ads. The tobacco industry spends 37 billion dollars per year on lobbying and advertising their products; yet smoking is the major factor in lung cancer deaths.

Medical knowledge has opened a new world of things women can do to protect themselves from breast cancer, from which 44,000 currently die each year — significantly lower than a decade ago. Obesity, diet, and smoking are associated with breast cancer. It remains the illness women worry about most, even though they are nine times more likely to die from heart disease. Every woman is at risk by being female. Now there are tests to determine high risk, taking only minutes to complete. A lot of women think that if they make 60 or 70 without getting breast cancer, they are home free. However, risk increases with age; the mean age of diagno-sis is 63.

<u>The Journal of the American Medical Association</u> reports a 76% lower risk of breast cancer among post-menopausal women tak-ing the drug *Raloxifene*. However, it is not risk free as it increases the chances of serious blood clots. One study of over 600 women who had breasts removed had their risk of dying reduced by 90%.

Women should have a Pap test annually to catch early warn-ing signs of cervical cancer after age 20 and a mammogram an-nually after age 40. Medicare now covers mammograms. A man whose breasts have enlarged or who finds a lump should also have a mammogram.

Prostate cancer among men is equal to the amount of breast cancer among women. For accuracy, a biopsy is more accurate than a rectal exam in diagnosis. The PSA test for prostate cancer should be done regularly for men over 50. If the PSA test is at 14, then

radiation or surgery is in order. An urologist, specializing in prostate problems, should do this major operation. Beyond age 70 physicians often don't operate but try to control the cancer with diet
and other treatments. It is a myth that treatments for prostate cancer leave men impotent and incontinent.

For cancer avoidance as well as for a healthy heart, we need to
eat green leafy vegetables, tomato and tomato products, lots of
orange juice, bean-packed dishes, and whole grained cereals.
Fiber in the outer layers of grains is often removed in processing.
Red grapefruit has almost 100 times more of the desirable beta-
carotene than white grapefruit. Green or black decaffeinated tea
is loaded with natural disease fighters. A word for green tea: it is
the least processed of teas and has the least amount of caffeine.
Calcium to strengthen from low fat milk and low fat cheese is
recommended. Studies also show that diets rich in olive oil reduce the risk of breast cancer.

Soy foods can block the effect of estrogen in breast cancer.
Chinese women who eat more soy have 80% less breast cancer
than American women. A substitute is flaxseed in the diet, which
also shrinks tumors. Bowel cancer is second to lung cancer in
occurrence. Stools with high fiber are softer and pass through
the body more quickly. The longer food is in the bowel, the longer
intestinal bacteria can create carcinogens. For both sexes a
colonoscopy every five years after 50 is recommended. Just consuming ten eight-ounce glasses of water each day, about three
more than normal, keeps urine diluted to flush away carcinogens. Any diet supplements should be taken only upon a doctor's
advice.

Researchers suspect that exercise's ability to bolster immunity may provide some protection against cancer in general. But exercise probably fights certain cancers in other ways as well. For example:

Colon cancer. Physical activity speeds the passage of waste materials through the colon, reducing its exposure to potentially cancer-causing compounds in the feces. Exercise also helps maintain low levels of the hormone insulin, which may stimulate the growth of colon cancer cells.

Breast cancer. The more estrogen in a woman's body during her lifetime, the greater her risk of breast cancer. Exercise inhibits production of pituitary hormones that trigger the release of estrogen during the menstrual cycle. Moreover, exercise can help reduce body fat, a secondary source of estrogen before menopause and the primary source afterward. (However, while weight-bearing exercise generally strengthens the bones, excessive exercise may reduce estrogen levels enough to weaken the bones and increase the risk of osteoporosis.)

Prostate cancer. Regular exercise may reduce levels of the male hormone testosterone in men, just as it reduces estrogen levels in women. And testosterone appears to fuel the growth of prostate cancer.

Skin cancer. Skin cancer is up due to overexposure to the sun, particularly between 10:00 a.m. and 2:00 p.m. Yet underexposure to sunlight in winter months in northern climes increases the risk of breast cancer, since about 90% of vitamin D is from ultraviolet light. For the skin any exposure to sun may be carcinogenic. The skin does not have to show red to be endangered. A tan indicates the skin has already been injured. Skin cancer now occurs more often than any other form of cancer. Most dermatologists recommend broad-spectrum sunblocks that filter both UVA and UVB rays. They should have a SPF (sun protection factor) of at least 30.

Most Americans precede the word "tan" with "healthy". The sun's rays are a cause of melanoma, the most serious form of skin cancer. Most melanoma can be cured if detected early. A yearly skin checkup is desirable. The sun's rays penetrate window glass, including car windows. They pass through water and are released from fluorescent and halogen light bulbs. Most people do not apply enough sunscreen. Better yet, when in the sun wear a hat with a brim at least three inches wide and protect your eyes with sunglasses because UV light can cause cataracts. Whenever possible cover the body with clothing.

In the new millennium much more will be learned about the two greatest killers: heart disease and cancer. Currently radiation, chemotherapy, and surgery are weapons to fight cancer. Being investigated is the use of laser (light) beams on the body to destroy early stages of cancer without surgery. Also in the cancer war are bone marrow and stem cell transplants. They require donors of stem cells and umbilical blood. Virtually all cancer deaths are preventable with good health practices, regular physical examinations, and use of existing medical procedures.

ENEMY NUMBER THREE: ALZHEIMER'S DISEASE

Due to people living longer, Alzheimer's has become a serious health problem. There are four million people with Alzheimer's. 14 million Americans will have AD by 2050 unless a cure or prevention is found. Alzheimer's can start at age 70, even earlier, and the chance doubles after age 85 with problems in space orientation, language, mood, and behaviors. With Alzheimer's one will live an average of eight years and possibly as many as 20 years or more. We have a 50% chance of living in a nursing home in very late life.

Neurologists can prescribe medications to reduce cell inflammation. Among them are *Cognex, Aricept*, heavy doses of vitamin E, and aspirin. A cure is several years away. With each new finding we move closer to designing treatments that delay, slow or even prevent the disease. When this is written, 50 to 60 drugs are in trials and approaching treatment, then approval, for use in treating Alzheimer's.

We all forget details as we age due to the vast amounts of data stored over a lifetime. Everyone over 60 can expect some minor memory loss that does not interfere with daily life. Our long-term memory is retained better than our short-term memory. The brain has ten million neurons with 60 trillion synapses located in five trillion cells to coordinate speech, sight, touch, smell, memory, and emotions.

Alzheimer's disease is not a normal part of aging. It is not losing one's keys; it is not remembering what the keys are for. Alzheimer's is getting lost on a walk in one's neighborhood. It is forgetting the name of one's favorite uncle. The disease is progressive as brain cells die and are not replaced. Sometimes symptoms are treatable or reversible. It is important to see a physician. Dementia may be associated with other diseases, such as stroke, Huntington's disease, or Parkinson's disease, whose symptoms are treatable. Almost one half of those over 85 show dementia in some form, but exact diagnosis is possible only with an autopsy. Physicians can now diagnose Alzheimer's with 80 to 90% accuracy with various tests.

It is normal to forget the day of the week or your destination for a moment. Alzheimer's is getting lost on one's own street, how to get there or how to get back home. One may also dress inappropriately, wearing several shirts or blouses. An Alzheimer's patient may place an iron in the freezer or a wristwatch in the sugar bowl. The disease can exhibit rapid mood changes — from calm to tears, to anger with no apparent reason. One can become extremely confused, suspicious, or fearful. There may be a loss of initiative, requiring prompting to become involved.

A physician's screen for dementia: The simple quiz below was designed by Dr. Marshall Folstein and several of his colleagues at Johns Hopkins to be administered as a quick and easy way to tell whether their patients are candidates for further diagnostic tests for possible dementias. Because there are so many variables involved (scores will depend on education levels, among other things), a correct interpretation of the final score must be left in the hands of a physician. The one general rule that applies is that most older people score above 25. Most likely, the quiz will seem very easy — further indication of the difference between ordinary forgetfulness and the extent of mental impairment that can result from actual dementia.

Maximum Points	Score	
		ORIENTATION
5	( )	1. What is the year, season, date, day, month? (1 point for each correct answer.)
5	( )	2. Where are we: state, county, street, house number? (1 point for each correct answer.)
		REGISTRATION
3	( )	3. Ask the person taking test to repeat a list of three objects you have named in the room. (1 point for each correct answer.)
		ATTENTION AND CALCULATION
5	( )	4. Have person count backwards by sevens from 100 (i.e. 100, 93, 86, 79, 72). Stop after five answers. Or, have him/her spell "world" backwards. (1 point for each correct number or letter.)
		RECALL
3	( )	5. Ask again for the three objects repeated above. (1 point for each correct answer.)
		LANGUAGE Instruct person to follow these commands:
9	( )	6. Name these two objects (hold up a pencil and a watch) (2 points)
	( )	7. Repeat the following: "no ifs, ands, or buts." (1 point.)
	( )	8. Take a paper in your right hand, fold it in half, and put it on the floor. (3 points.)
	( )	9. Close your eyes. (1point.)
	( )	10. Write a sentence (it must be grammatical, with a subject, verb, and predicate.) (1 point.)
	( )	11. Copy the figure below. (1 point.)

Total score: _____

Senility

Forgetting is not necessarily a sign of senility. According to the National Institute on aging, senility is "not even a disease," and the term should not be used, as it commonly is, to cover everything from Alzheimer's disease to more widespread and reversible conditions that mimic symptoms of Alzheimer's, such as memory loss. Memory problems are eminently treatable when triggered by minor head injuries, high fever, poor nutrition, adverse reactions to medication, or the emotional problems common to old age — depression, loneliness, boredom.

Memory loss in Alzheimer's disease is irreversible, however, though it is benign in the early stages — when victims begin to forget appointments or friends' names. For the percentage of the population over 65 who will come down with Alzheimer's, it is the apparent triviality of those early symptoms that provokes anxiety among the not-so-silent majority of the "normally" forgetful.

A caregiver staying at home with someone with severe dementia can get relief by hiring a buddy to come in for limited hours. These geriatric care managers charge by the hour. Then there are adult care centers where the person affected can be dropped off in the morning and picked up in the afternoon. These centers allow the patient to continue to live at home and still give family members their lives back, permitting time for business affairs, rest, and associations with their peers. If finally necessary, a retirement facility with a special dementia unit or a nursing home is an option.

For relief, continued regular exercise increases blood flow to the brain. Also puzzle solving helps build brain connector dendrites. An herbal product Ginkgo is reported to show modest gains but in high doses is a blood thinner. Vitamins C and E, beta-carotene, and selenium can be added to the list. A neurologist should be consulted before using any drugs or over-the-counter medications.

The common causes of ordinary memory troubles include anxiety, fatigue, stress, grief, and mild depression. In addition, an illness, isolation, habitual inactivity, limitations of vision or hearing, and excessive use of alcohol can all induce memory loss. The importance of a good diet and regular exercise, having a regular physical examination, and willingness to accept new challenges cannot be overemphasized. To assist the aging brain, we use calendars, appointment books, and to-do lists. Keep keys in the same place at all times and use an expandable wristband to hold constantly needed keys. Reading, writing, interacting with friends, and travel if possible help us keep mentally alert. Eliminating distractions and background and taking occasional breaks can aid in keeping the mind fresh.

Exercising Your Memory

Mnemonics, the art of improving short-term recall and ferreting out stored facts, depends on strong visual images and meaningful associations: it's a system for cross-indexing stored information in interesting ways. These methods take only a little time to master. They work because they seize the attention and demand concentration. The more outrageous the connections we set up, the better.

Use *loci* (Latin for places). Take a string of facts to be remembered: for instance, points you want to cover in a talk. Match each one to a specific site you can visualize easily — your living room, perhaps, or your street. If you're giving a talk on substance abuse, make a tour of the living room, stationing your introductory remarks on drug cartels on the table left of the fireplace. On the mantel, store what you're planning to say about government policy. To the right of the fireplace, in the bookcase, situate drug education — and so forth, around the room. When you give your talk, make another mental tour of the room and "pick up" your notes. You can adopt the same *loci* to something more innocuous, like a grocery list: pasta on the table, tomato sauce on the mantel, salad greens in the bookcase.

Make up rhymes. Nobody ever forgets the useful "I before E, except after C." But to remember home chores make up your own rhymes: "Skitty, skat, let in the cat," for instance. The cornier the better.

Compose mental pictures, particularly when you're trying to remember a name: Helen Decker, say, might conjure up a vision of Helen of Troy on shipboard.

Repeat or rehearse new facts. "How do you do, Helen," you say when introduced at a party. A few minutes later you say to yourself, "That's Helen Decker." And a minute or so after that, "Can I get you anything to drink, Helen?" You probably won't forget Helen's name.

Make up acronyms or sentences. "Maple" could help an out-of-towner in New York City remember the order of Madison, Park, and Lexington Avenues. "The postman at Sutter's Mill was bushed from pining for California" could help a visitor remember the order of five San Francisco streets, Post, Sutter, Bush, Pine, and California.

Chunk or regroup clusters of data to give them a pattern. Telephone numbers are already partially grouped, but you can give them further meaning. Helen's three-number exchange, 744, is easy to remember, but you won't forget the rest of the number either, 4591, when you reflect that she looks to be about 45, almost halfway to 91.

Write things down. Writing notes and making lists will often fix things in your mind. You may not even have to refer to your notes or lists.

Structure your life. Even the hook for the house keys by the back door is a mnemonic device: you always look there first. Similarly, keep your checkbook in the drawer of your desk, or park your reading glasses on the night table.

Ease your mind. If you feel your are forgetting too much, consider the following:

- Give yourself time. The sky won't fall in if you forget a name or a number, and if you employ a few delaying tactics (don't rush up to a friend whose name you've forgotten); the missing data may surface. If they don't, don't make a big fuss over it. Just admit you've forgotten.
- Don't expect too much. If you're nervous about forgetting, you usually do.
- Play games. Crossword puzzles, Scrabble, and card games are all good exercises for improving memory.
- Improve your mind. Going to lectures, taking classes, and joining groups will introduce new stimuli and keep your neurons transmitting.

As we age, we may seek a simpler life style. The author at 85 has moved to a quality retirement home in a college town. Many wait so long to choose retirement housing they are incapacitated when they move in. They miss out on living arrangements that are becoming state of the art for retirement living. Stair climbing is passé. Safety measures are built-in, as near as a pull cord for the immediate availability of trained help. These homes offer one, two, or three meal options; a one meal requirement allows a daily check on one's viability. Available opportunities and services are in-house libraries with special rotating collections, crafts, art, woodworking, and exercise equipment, scheduled house cleaning service, visiting lecturers, classic movies, religious services, holiday and birthday parties, writing classes, a computer room, a game room, travelogues, an in-house newsletter, live musical performances, transportation at the door for shopping, guided vacation trips and rides in the country, and walking paths in a natural setting.

A diverse group of entrepreneurs is entering the continuing care business due to the growing aging population. More than a few of these are skimming profits off with high entrance fees and then in a few years filing for bankruptcy having bled the institution's reserve funds. In a guaranteed life care facility one will never have to move. The complex of apartments has an attached or on-grounds nursing center, an acute care center, and a dementia unit.

Of the 5,000 and rapidly growing number of retirement homes, only 10%, about 500, have the highest rating — accreditation as a certified Continuing Care Retirement Community. (CCRC) These usually have four levels of care on one campus; one is guaranteed lifetime care even if one's finances run out. One time entrance fees range from $50,000 to over $100,000. These non-profit facilities have on-site management and volunteer citizens' boards of directors.

Types of Living Arrangements:

Independent Garden Apartment

Complete independent living
Grounds care outside
Available nursing

One to Three Room Apt.

1,2, or 3 meals in a formal
dining room
Weekly linen service and
housekeeping
Available nursing

Assisted Living

Own apartment, 24 hour staff
Medicines administrated
Bathing and dressing help
Housekeeping and personal
laundry done

Nursing

24 hour nursing care
Dietitian
Physical, etc. therapies
available
Activity programs

Considerations in choosing a retirement facility are suggested. Do residents look happily involved in activities and not just staring into space? Is the dining room attractive and are there homelike lounge areas for conversation? Is there a schedule of activities in rooms provided and is there an adequate library? Do apartments have small kitchens, a bath tub with grab bars, and an emergency cord in each room? Is there strong participation by residents in in-house movies, outside lecturers, entertainers, and musicians? Are the residents involved in self-government? Are guest rooms available? Is public transportation nearby? Does the home provide their own buses for shopping, medical visits, and travel tours? Is there an interdenominational chaplain or counselor on the staff? Are there a gift shop, a beauty shop, and a handicraft workshop? Is there an opportunity for residents to plant gardens?

Some accredited Continuing Care Retirement Communities are provided as examples:

Asbury Methodist Village, Gaithersburg, MD
                          (near Washington, D.C.)
Glacier Hills, Ann Arbor, Michigan
Casa Dorinda, Santa Barbara, California
Plymouth Harbor, Sarasota, Florida

In late age, most of us experience some loss of short-term memory and possibly a diminishment of the ability to learn and respond quickly. We can, however, learn to work around these losses.

Infirmity does not have to follow old age. People in their 90s and 100s can still maintain independence if they follow a fitness program. Walking, some weight training, and low impact aerobics can keep us relaxed, comfortable, and flexible. Diet choices are an important aspect of long life. Thus far Alzheimer's cannot be prevented, but eating less saturated fat and high calorie foods and more green vegetables and fruits, along with reducing sodium, can lessen the risk of stroke leading to dementia. And by all means, no smoking!

Mental exercise is as important as physical exercise. We can't just sit out the Golden Years. We can keep learning. We can regularly be researching an interest.

We must not remain socially and emotionally isolated. By socializing, we ask for help and give help, volunteering and keeping involved. The new challenge is make 60 to 100+ among the best years of our lives surrounded by friends and absorbing interests.

ENEMY NUMBER FOUR: INFLUENZA AND COLDS

Influenza

Influenza is now under better control, but 40,000 Americans still die from the disease each year. Doctors still get calls from older patients complaining of shortness of breath, fever, aches and pains, and severe chills. People at high risk for the flu and its complications are those with any of the following conditions:

- Chronic lung disease
- Heart disease
- Chronic kidney disease
- Diabetes and other chronic metabolic disorders
- Severe anemia
- Depressed immunity resulting from various diseases or treatments

Anyone can be exposed from another's cough, from handling objects, or from breathing recycled air, as on an airplane. In a single cough a million particles of the flu virus can fill the air. Cigarette smoking and excessive alcohol consumption can impair swallowing, allowing mouth germs to be aspirated into the lungs. As this book goes to press, new drugs to prevent flu contagion are being announced. There are safe vaccines for this disease that circle the globe each year in a new form. These vaccines, covered by Medicare, are advised and administered in the fall.

Pneumonia, lung inflammation or infection, which can be either viral or bacterial, has a vaccine too. Pneumonia vaccine whose protection lasts more than one year is advisable for all older people who can be susceptible to flu complications. For those with chronic illnesses, recovering from a severe illness, in a nursing home or other chronic care facility should also receive a once in a lifetime injection of a vaccine for bacterial pneumococcal pneumonia.

Colds

Viruses — about two hundred different varieties — cause colds. Antibiotics are no help unless complications include some sort of bacterium. Here are suggestions for preventing colds or treating them when escape is unavoidable. Colds are not passed through the air, only through physical touch. If you are around someone with a cold, keep your hands clean by washing them frequently. Keep at least three feet away from coughers and sneezers and avoid buildings with poor air circulation and low humidity, from which cold viruses cannot escape. You can flush germs from the body by drinking plenty of fluids. Again, keep to a proper varied diet and get regular exercise. If you are around someone with a cold, avoid touching your nose and eyes. Equally important, dispose of used tissues promptly: discard them in a plastic-lined wastebasket or paper bag, or in any manner that makes rehandling them unnecessary. Don't share drinking and eating utensils, telephones, and other objects with family members who have colds. Use liquid soap from a dispenser instead of bar soaps. Paper towels and paper cups for the bathroom also make sense.

If you should catch a cold, with a scratchy throat, watery eyes, and a stuffed-up head; you should stay at home, get plenty of rest, and increase moisture in the air. Though nothing really cures a cold, some of the common sense home remedies do help:

• Gargling with warm salt water soothes a sore throat.

• Scientific studies have shown that hot drinks, especially chicken soup, can increase the flow of nasal secretions and help you feel better. The taste and aroma of the soup, as well as its hot vapors, may all be part of the therapy. Soup is also packed with protein, vitamins, and minerals.

• Tea with honey often brings relief to a sore throat.

Drink plenty of water and take an aspirin or two for aches and pains. Extra vitamins C and E may help reduce a cold's severity. Researchers at the Cleveland Clinic have run tests on zinc lozenges; if sucked on during the first 24 hours of a cold, they often result in fewer days of coughing, sneezing, and drippy noses. Use over-the-counter remedies only in moderation. Always contact your physician promptly if you have earache, pain in the face or forehead, a temperature above 102 degrees, persistent hoarseness, shortness of breath, or a dry, painful cough.

To emphasize, for cold prevention stay away from crowds. There are billions of colds each year and still no immediate cure. A retiree with a cold probably can stay at home the week the cold needs to run its course. If the cold persists after ten days, it is time to consult your doctor.

OTHER ENEMIES: ARTHRITIS, OSTEOPOROSIS, AND PARKINSON'S DISEASE

Arthritis involves inflammation or damage to the joints. It is most common in late life, affecting 80% of individuals, more women than men. The most common is osteoarthritis, a hardening or stiffening of the spinal column or other large weight-bearing joints, such as the hips or knees. Rheumatoid arthritis is a chronic disease of the joints characterized by alternating periods of active inflammation and absence of symptoms, both of variable duration. Hands and feet are most often affected, but the disease may occur in wrists, knees, ankles, or neck. It is found more rarely in the spine or hips. Only one in ten with rheumatoid arthritis is severely disabled. It is a permanent but usually manageable condition. Obesity raises the risk of both types of arthritis. Morning stiffness for osteoarthritis usually lasts only a few minutes. By contrast, with rheumatoid arthritis, the morning stiffness can last for hours.

Exercise helps lessen the pain and increases movement in joints that are affected, reduces fatigue, and helps us look and feel better. There are three main types of exercises:

- Range-of-motion exercises move a joint as far as it will comfortably go — then stretch it a little farther.
- Strength training increases or maintains our muscle strength without moving our joints.
- Endurance activities build overall fitness, keep our hearts healthy and control our weight.

Plan exercise for the time of day with the least amount of stiffness and pain. Try to aim for a goal of 30 minutes a day, five or six days a week. Hot baths, showers, and heat packs relax sore muscles and relieve joint pain.

A physician will likely prescribe a nonsteroidal anti-inflammatory drug or even prescriptive medications. Since rheumatoid arthritis is a disorder of the immune system, in some cases to reduce antibodies in the blood, a physician may prescribe chemotherapy (anticancer) drugs.

Osteoporosis means "holes in the bones", reducing bone density. With age, bones fracture more easily. Most debilitating are fractures of bones in the spinal column or hips. Dietary calcium intake is important at all ages. Calcium supplements may be prescribed for those with osteoporosis. Besides building strong bones and maintaining bone density and strength, calcium also plays a role in regulating the heartbeat and other vital functions. The daily recommended dietary allowance, or RDA, is 800 milligrams daily. Many experts recommend that postmenopausal women consume at least 1,500 milligrams. A cup of milk provides 300 milligrams of calcium, eight ounces of yogurt, 300 to 450 milligrams.

Compression of spinal bones can give a humped-over appearance. It is more common in older women as a consequence of reproductive hormone deficiency. Estrogen replacement therapy can be effective, but not for women at high risk for cancer or have had cancer. *Raloxifene* is a drug approved to fight osteoporosis.

For osteoporosis both heat and ice relieve pain. For arthritis, using a cane and wearing running shoes can help relieve strain on a joint. To get the most benefit from a cane, find one the correct height, holding it in the hand opposite the affected joint. When standing, the top of the cane should come to the level of the crease between the wrist and the lower arm.

Keeping flexible with moderate exercise and bed and tool modifications is helpful for those with joint and bone diseases. Water exercise, because water supports much of the body's weight, allows movement without stressing the joints. Warm water itself is therapeutic.

Back Exercises

Use these exercises to help prevent back pain; if you've had pain, wait until you are pain-free to begin. Begin slowly, build up gradually, and back off if you experience pain. Hold each position for a count of 10, then exhale and relax. Repeat each exercise 3 times, then build to 8-10 repetitions. Do your exercises 3-4 times per week. Consult a physical therapist or physician if you have chronic or recurrent back pain.

These are best done on a firm surface such as the floor, a straight chair, or a very firm bed.

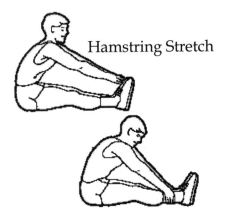

Hamstring Stretch

Sitting Back Bend

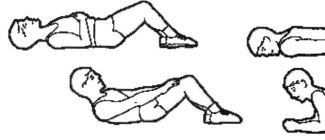

Half Sit-up

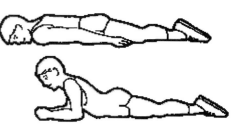

Elbow Prop-up

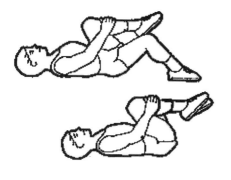

Knee to Chest Raise

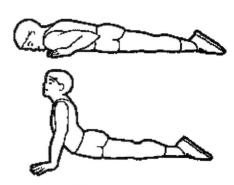

Press-up

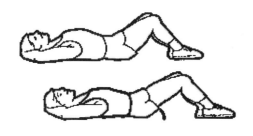

Pelvic Tilt

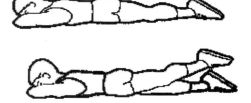

Hip Hyperextension

When standing:
1. Keep your head level and your chin slightly tucked in.
2. Stand tall, stretching the top of your head toward the ceiling.
3. Relax your shoulders.
4. Tighten your stomach muscles to tuck in your stomach. This will help prevent excessive swayback, or lordosis, in the lower part of your back.

When sitting:
1. Keep your head level and chin up.
2. Keep your buttocks to the back of the chair and maintain a slight inward curve in your lower back. Sometimes a small pillow or rolled towel in the small of the back helps. Do not slouch.
3. Keep your feet comfortably apart and supported so that your knees are level with your hips.

When lying or sleeping:
1. Use a firm mattress.
2. Lie on your side with your hips and knees slightly bent and with a pillow between your legs.
3. Lie on your stomach with a pillow under your head and one under your ankles.
4. If you find you are able to sleep only on your back, a pillow under your knees may take the strain off your lower back.

When lifting:

1. Keep your head level and your chin up.
2. Keep your back straight, bend your knees and squat as low as possible, keeping your feet apart.
3. Lift with the strength of your legs.
4. Never twist or turn while lifting.
5. Once you've picked up the object, hold it close to you.

Beds and Tools

Pillows: Bad sleeping position is a common cause of aches and pains. If you have a stiff neck or shoulder most mornings, try a different pillow. New pillows can be expensive, and no one pillow is going to answer everyone's needs. Ideally, your neck should be straight most of the night. Some foam pillows are too high and firm, or too bouncy. Some down pillows are too soft and flat. If you generally sleep on your back or side, you might benefit from a "cervical roll", a small round pillow for neck support. This can be easily used by itself or in addition to your regular pillow. If your mattress is very firm and you sleep on your side, you may need a thicker pillow than you would on a mattress that allows your shoulder to sink into it. If you sleep on your stomach most of the night, try a soft, oversized pillow that goes under your chest but supports your head and neck. Try sleeping with different pillows or combinations of pillows. Or simply try a rolled-up towel as a cervical pillow. Some people prefer no pillow at all.

Bed wedges. These help you stay comfortable while reading or watching TV in bed. If you sleep on your back, you can also use a wedge to elevate your knees in order to relieve pressure on the disks in your lower back.

Bed boards. You can firm up a sagging mattress (a frequent contributor to back pain) by placing a board between it and the box spring. Lightweight folding models are available for travel.

"Back-saving" tools. One type of snow shovel or rake has a bent handle that allows you to stand nearly upright while working, thus reducing stress on the lower back. Lightweight shovels can also help. Some shoehorns have an extra-long handle so you don't have to bend over when putting on shoes. Long-handled grips and hooks are available to help reach or manipulate objects above your reach.

Falls

With aging the likelihood of falling increases. For example, using a large number of medications can increase the risk of falls. There are strategies for preventing falls. Use stairs with care. Installed handrails need to extend beyond the last step. Nonskid treads can be applied on the steps. Four out of five accidents occur when descending steps. Installing grab bars in a bathtub or shower, along with a small stool to aid in bathing, are other measures to prevent falls. In winter use only walkways clear of ice and snow.

Shoes should have flat rubber soles, pants should reach above the heel, and we should avoid walking around the house in socks, stockings, or slippers that allow us to slip. Canes, walkers, and wheelchairs need to be adjusted to our height and worn rubber tips replaced. We can have our eyes and ears checked annually. Inactivity and social isolation also make the body weaken, increasing the risk of falling.

Parkinson's disease affects around one and one-half million people in the United States. It is caused by a gradual deterioration of certain nerve centers within the brain, those coordinating movement. Thus, tremors, stiffness, and loss of spontaneous movement occur. The cause is still unknown; research is directed to slowing the progression of the degenerative process. Drugs to balance dopamine and acetylcholine within the affected brain area are usually prescribed. *Levodopa* with *Carbidopa* and *Benzthiazide* to reduce side effects can reduce symptoms in three of four patients. New drugs are constantly being researched; nothing yet has been proven completely effective against the tremors of the disease or its progression. A new drug, *Cinemax*, is being tested, and new surgical techniques are being tried. For many patients, drug treatments enable them to remain independent longer, and they are able to live out a normal life span.

Physical therapy with muscle-strengthening exercises can help. These include exercises for speaking, swallowing, and overall muscle tone. Exercises do not stop progression of the disease but may permit the patient to be less disabled by movement problems by keeping motor functions at an optimum level.

Parkinson's disease has affected Pope John Paul II, the dancer Martha Graham, prizefighter Muhammad Ali, and many others. Janet Reno, Attorney General of the U.S., does nothing to hide her tremors. She dismisses them as "phantom wings" and makes her condition a part of her everyday life.

OVERLOOKED ONE-THIRD OF LIFE: SLEEP RENEWAL

Close to two-thirds of Americans get less than the recommended eight hours of sleep each night. Bed is not the place to read, to watch television, or to use the telephone. But going to bed at the same time and arising at the same time is a rewarding habit. In later life one has more freedom in selecting the time for sleep. One good pattern is from 10:00 p.m. to 6:00 a.m.

In general, a sleep cycle lasts about 90 to 110 minutes, during which time we progress through five stages. As we drift off, we enter Stage 1, a NREM (non-rapid eye movement) phase. As we fall deeper asleep, we move to Stages 2 through 4 (all NREM phases). Then we enter Stage 5, the REM deep, dreaming phase. After this, we cycle back to NREM Stage 2 (not all the way to Stage 1) and begin a new sleep cycle.

To avoid light and hasten sleep, a mask for the eyes (found at a local drug store) can be useful. A director of sleep at Emory University suggests drinking a glass of warm water to shorten the time needed to fall asleep. Most people sleep best at a 60 to 65 degree temperature, preferably with fresh air coming into the room. We should refrain from drinking coffee, any beverage containing caffeine, or alcohol within four hours of bedtime. We may think drinks induce sleep, but there is likely to be a rebound effect in a few hours. Elders should limit alcohol to one drink daily. In aging, because of the shift of the ratio of body fat to body water, alcohol has about twice the effect on seniors as it does on young adults.

If a cigarette smoker, we should avoid smoking in the evening since nicotine is a stimulant. Best of all, stop smoking completely for good sleep and overall health. We should avoid strenuous exercise two hours or more before bedtime, although daytime exercise helps us sleep. Some find counting sheep creates calmness for sleep. Others try to relax each muscle group, progressing slowly from the toes to the head. It is best not to nap after 3:00 p.m.

If we can't get to sleep after 20 minutes, we may choose to get up and move to another room, do some deep breathing to clear the mind, to listen to soothing music, or read for awhile. Upon returning to bed, we may cover our eyes with our eye shade, after checking the room temperature and the fresh air. Only a doctor should prescribe sleeping pills.

Chronic insomnia that lasts longer than four weeks usually means that there is a serious underlying medical condition. For example, insomnia can be a symptom of heart disease or thyroid disease.

Certain medications can be detrimental to sleep. Some over-the-counter drugs have a stimulant effect. Prescription drugs that can cause sleep disturbance include some antidepressants, blood pressure-lowering drugs, heart medications, thyroid medications, and steroids.

A major cause of chronic insomnia is depression. People who are depressed often either sleep too much or have trouble sleeping.

Anyone with a sleep problem should see his or her physician. We all need adequate sleep within a regular pattern. Renewal from sleep gives us a jump-start on each new day.

HEARING AND VISION IN AGING

Our ears' function is to pick up sounds and conduct them to the inner ear. The outer and middle ear are designed with amazing skill and efficiency to perform this function — our ears are sensitive to wide ranges of sound frequency and intensity. However, all kinds of conductive problems can develop. Hearing problems are fairly prevalent among the older population in the United States. About one-third of Americans between 65 and 74 and one-half of those aged 85 years and older have hearing problems. These problems can be as insignificant as missing certain sounds to total deafness.

Most common for the aging is "old hearing" — involving some changes in the inner ear and brain, but can also involve conductive impairment, in which the bones of the middle ear become stiff or the eardrum becomes thicker and less flexible. These changes may reflect less blood supply to the ear as a result of heart disease, high blood pressure, or other circulatory problems.

Some ways to tell whether you have a hearing problem:
- Words are difficult to understand, as if slurred or mumbled (especially if it gets worse when there is background noise).
- Certain sounds are overly annoying or loud.
- A hissing or ringing in the background is heard.
- Television shows, concerts, or parties are less enjoyable because you can't hear much.
- You must strain to understand conversations.
- Other people do not seem to speak clearly.

Sometimes people find it difficult to admit they are having trouble hearing. They may become more isolated to avoid the frustration of not understanding what is being spoken. As a result, the problem may be ignored and untreated, making the problem worse.

Help is available, including special training, lip reading, hearing aids, medicines and/or surgery. There are numerous kinds of hearing aids: tiny ones that fit inside the ear, some larger that also fit inside the ear, some that fit behind the ear, and some that include a battery pack with buttons to adjust for any room or social situation. Most important is being tested by an audiologist upon referral from your physician to determine the best remedy for your particular problem. If a hearing aid is recommended, then it is up to you to use it!

Vision problems can occur at all ages, but some are more pronounced in older people. Most important is having a complete eye examination with a specialist every one or two years. Most eye problems can be corrected, especially if they are diagnosed early.

Developing cataracts is one eye problem most commonly occurring as we age. A cataract is the clouding of the normal transparent, clear lens in the eye. This may develop over many years, maybe in one eye only, maybe just partially clouding the lens. Symptoms include the following:
- Blurred or double vision.
- Sensitivity to light and glare, making driving difficult.
- Less vivid perception of color.
- Frequent eyeglass prescription changes.

We should consider removal when a cataract is interfering with our work, hobbies, or lifestyle. Surgery means a lens replacement, either an intraocular lens that will be permanent or a removable contact lens, or glasses, or a combination. Cataract surgery is now over 90% successful in restoring useful vision.

Glaucoma is one of the leading causes of blindness. Two of 100 people over 35 have vision threatened by glaucoma. When diagnosed early, blindness is almost always preventable. Glaucoma is pressure on the optic nerve, due to the blocked flow of the aqueous humor normally flowing continually throughout parts of the inner eye, (like a blocked drainage system). Regular eye examinations are extremely important to detect this disease! The condition is treated with eye drops several times a day or occasionally pills. The condition may change suddenly; thus, frequent follow-up examinations are important to possibly adjust the treatment or change the treatment if side effects are present. Surgery may sometimes be necessary. With prompt diagnosis, this disease can be controlled.

Macular degeneration is an eye disease that involves damage or breakdown of the macula, a small area where light rays are focused on the retina at the back of the eye. The macula's size is approximately the size of this O. A blurred area occurs as in the center of a camera picture, thus affecting reading or close work. 70% of patients have involutional macular degeneration, associated with aging, for which there is no cure. Another 10% have exudative macular degeneration, caused by leaking or broken blood vessels at the back of the eye. If done early, surgery can help patients with the exudative type. Other varieties may occur from injury, infection, or inflammation. This disease may affect only one eye at a time.

Typical symptoms are these:

- Words on a page look blurred.
- Straight lines are distorted, often more so in the center of vision.
- A dark or empty area appears in the center of vision.

Bright illumination, special lamps, magnifying aids, closed circuit television, Large Print books and newspapers may be of help to those with macular degeneration.

To diagnose and treat hearing and eye problems early is of utmost importance. Regular physical examinations are essential!

BEATING STRESS AND DEPRESSION: LAUGH AND BE HEALTHY

Two-thirds of visits to doctors may stem from stress-related elements, such as fatigue, headaches, excessive worry, and depression. Chronic dissatisfaction, bitterness, frustration, anger, and envy are harbingers of untimely aging. Counterfactors are friends, family, and simplifying our lives. Goal setting helps conserve energy. Learning to say no, not trying to do everything ourselves, letting others assist on occasion is healthful. Relaxation and vacations are as important as being busy.

STRESS SELF-EVALUATION

Instructions: Read each statement and write the number which you think best characterizes yourself and your behavior at the present time. There are no right or wrong answers. Try not to spend too much time over each answer.

1. Not at all **2.** Slightly **3.** Moderately **4.** Very much

Answers

1. I often lose my appetite or eat when I'm not hungry......... (   )
2. My decisions tend to be more impulsive than planned;
   I tend to feel unsure about my choices and change my
   mind often..(   )
3. The muscles of my neck, back or stomach
   frequently get tense..(   )
4. I have thoughts and feelings about my problems that
   run through my mind for much of the time.......................(   )
5. I have a hard time getting to sleep, wake up often
   or feel tired..(   )

6. I feel the urge to cry or to escape and get away from my problems...( )
7. I tend to let anger build up and then explosively release my temper in some aggressive or destructive act.............( )
8. I have nervous habits (tapping my fingers, shaking my leg, pulling my hair, scratching, wringing my hands, etc.) ......( )
9. I often feel fatigued, even when I have not been doing hard physical work...( )
10. I have regular problems with constipation, diarrhea, upset stomach or nausea..( )
11. I tend to not meet my expectations, either because they are unrealistic, or I have taken on more of a burden than I can handle..( )
12. I periodically lose my interest in sex................................( )
13. My anger gets aroused easily...( )
14. I often have bad, unhappy dreams or nightmares...........( )
15. I tend to spend a great deal of time worrying about things..( )
16. My use of alcohol, coffee, drugs or tobacco has increased..( )
17. I feel anxious, often without any reason that I can identify..( )
18. In conversation my speech tends to be weak, rapid, broken or tense..( )
19. I tend to be short-tempered and irritable with people.....( )
20. Delays, even ordinary ones, make me fiercely impatient ....( )

Finding 3s and 4s above, we can set goals to overcome them.

Not all stress can be avoided.   How we react or respond is what counts. Some negatives may lead to positives. It is what we do with what happens to us that makes the difference. Overcoming a physical problem or dealing successfully with a family emergency are examples.

We can slow breathing rate with deep instead of shallow breaths that will divert oxygen-carrying blood to all areas of the body and especially to the heart and circulatory system. To assist deep breathing we use the diaphragm, the stomach muscles, the rib cage, and the lower back. We can curb the effects of stress by exercise and diet. We can also find solace in nature, turning to friends to share, and seeking help from meditation and spiritual resources.

Finding laughter in stressful situations is a great releaser of body tensions, preventing and even healing disease. Laughter boosts the immune system and brings a host of physical changes in the brain. When ill, Norman Cousins, author of *Anatomy of an Illness*, rented a pile of comedy videos, watching them every day and just letting himself laugh. Other activities for release of stress are socializing, physical activity, hobby projects, and further education.

Here's a HEALTHY OUTLOOK TEST:
    Answer each with a yes or no.

1. I see friends regularly.
2. I am an optimist and can find laughter in many situations.
3. I find new challenges to replace defeats.

4. Spirituality and faith make a difference in my life.
5. Alternatives to negatives can lead to positives.
6. Some amount of stress gives me energy.
7. I exercise and control diet as counters to stress.
8. I control stress. I am a mediator.
9. I am alert to new information, to group therapy.
10. In sleep I lie on my side and get full renewal.
11. I like where I live, my family, and my friends.
12. I set new goals, make changes, learn to let go.

Stress can be reduced by careful time management in a world that becomes ever more fast-paced. We can consult freely the health information in our local public library and nearest hospital library. We can find community support groups for sharing almost anything in our local newspapers. On the Internet there is help — *WWW.Mastering Stress.com.* Everyone feels low occasionally. We should strive to make these lows temporary.

Real depression among the elderly rarely gets treated. It is an illness, not a weakness to hide. A medical examination, with a possible referral to a specialist, is the route to go. Depression can be overcome with medication and/or therapy.

Remember that some stress may be stimulating and good for us. Everyone gets down in the dumps now and then; but older adults can gear their lives toward maximizing the positive and minimizing the negative. Once in awhile we should satisfy an urge to do something entirely different and out of the ordinary. Acting upon "whims", we heal ourselves. Remember, we can often learn to deal with a really big problem by giving ourselves a heavy dose of hearty laughter.

ROAD RAGE AND SAFETY

Two cars in a family are becoming passé. In Tucson builders are offering five and six-car garages, approaching the space allocated to the rest of the house. The four-car garage is going national as we seek residential paradise. Farmland and woodlands are divided into five-acre plots. Neighborhoods with front porches for greeting passersby have nearly disappeared. Lost forever are downtowns with main street shopping. Now malls line the freeways instead. The average drive to a job is now six miles. For some, commuting one or two hours a day is common.

Crowded freeways are making rural America a memory in many parts of the country. Gridlock on highways and air pollution follow, along with increasing road rage. To save time, drivers scoot back and forth for position and the margin for error increases. Speed is the chief cause of crashes that kill thousands each year. For each increase of five miles per hour, kinetic energy goes up 45%. An additional factor is that the federal Department of Transportation estimates that traffic will increase 50% by 2008.

To reduce crowded traffic, higher density in towns and cities could provide stores and offices on ground floors and apartments above with sidewalks and small parks for strolling with mass transit stops nearby. BART in San Francisco, a high-speed rail service, is an example of a good transit system. Other cities have good computer-coordinated bus systems.

A growing hazard is the heavy trucks with up to forty wheels that now deliver up to 90% of the freight in the United States. Their advantage over rail travel is door-to-door delivery. Let it be said that truck drivers generally are well-trained and are very efficient; however, these trucks are beginning to fill our interstate highways. Some are doubles with a carrier hitched to the back. Their speed limit is 55 miles per hour, but finding them at that speed is getting rarer. Yet with more commuters squeezed onto highways, additional road construction has increased only 1% in thirteen years.

With 207 million cars and three and one-half million trucks, what can be done to increase safety? The present vehicle market is primarily for sports vehicles and pick-up trucks that contribute to congested streets and highways. They are so tall that they block the forward view of regular sized cars in bumper to bumper traffic. Also due to their heavier weight, they are harder to turn and easier to turn over. The major problems for car drivers are following too closely, lane change violations, and speed violations — all of which can contribute to a crash by either cars or trucks. Other problems are drivers using cell telephones conducting business in three states, writing notes, or flossing their teeth while going down the road! Even carrying on a conversation with passengers can be a distraction for the driver.

Drivers over 75 are three times more likely than those younger to be involved in a fatal auto crash. Factors are failure to yield right of way; turning left or right across lanes of traffic; not double-checking before entering traffic; not seeing and obeying all road signs and signals; and health problems, such as poor vision and poor attention span. Yet there is no magic age at which we should stop driving. Attending a review driving training class is helpful.

Some people in their late 80s perform well. In our 90s, it may be a different ball game. Taxis and public transportation are available. If we continue to drive, we should carry on the back of our driver's license our doctor's name, address, and telephone number; our blood type; a list of our medications; and the name and telephone number of our next of kin. In an accident insist on a police report, without which one's insurance does not pay.

We can regularly review our driving habits. A wide angle rearview mirror and an additional curved mirror attached to the driver's outside mirror pick up a car approaching on the immediate left when we are contemplating a lane change. A safety measure under development is an automatic adaptation of cruise control, warning if we are too close to another vehicle. To follow another car at a safe distance, pick out a road marker ahead and count two seconds between your car and the car ahead. Check weekly for recommended tire pressure and take your car in for regular maintenance.

Never pull off to the left when leaving the road; go off to the right. Care is needed in a sudden rainfall: water plus oil and dirt on the road combine to make a slick film. If a tailgater doesn't refrain when you tap the brakes, pull over to let him pass. One always has a blind spot one car length on either side. Use the turn signal well in advance and take a quick glance over your shoulder before making a move. Try to avoid a situation calling for slamming on the brakes to avoid a skid. Pedestrians have the right of way, even if they are in the wrong place at the wrong time. Finally, our eyes adjust more slowly as we age; night driving should be limited or eliminated.

LOOKING TO THE FUTURE

In older years we are entitled to enjoy new freedoms. There is more time to enjoy sunrises, sunsets, and midday calm sitting in the shade. We can find good books to read, carefully selected television programs, educational radio, and the Internet bringing the world into our living rooms. At age 98 Ella Stump felt arthritis was killing her. Reversing course at age 103 she has mastered word processing and written two books.

In the new century women are coming into their own to make a difference. There is a growing club of women presidents: President Mary Aleese in Ireland, President Ruth Dreifuss in Switzerland, President Mireya Moscoso in Panama, President Janet Jagan in Guyana, Prime Minister Jenny Shipley in New Zealand, and Hasina Wajed in Bangladesh. These women are breaking ground for a woman to become President of the United States.

A McArthur study reports that with training we can improve cognitive functions. At over age 100 Rose Friedman paints, takes Spanish lessons, and wears a suit and high heels almost every day. Eleanor Roosevelt said, "Aging now offers us time to do things we thought we couldn't do." She called it "Senior Power". From 1950 it took until 2000 for knowledge to double. By 2020 doubling is expected to occur every two and one-half months. It is worth waiting for.

We see the world getting smaller each year. At the beginning of the new century Amtrak is operating a 150-mile per hour train system between Boston and Washington, D.C. Similar trains are to follow in the Great Lakes, The Gulf Coast, California, and the Pacific Northwest. No longer will we have to wait an hour and twenty minutes for our luggage after deplanning. On the train luggage is kept nearby. Rail transit is a tour of the landscape in a roomy seat with an available dining car and a sleeping car for going cross-country. Already underway is a monster railroad linking Alaska to the lower 48 states, going from Fairbanks through Whitehorse in the Yukon Territory to Prince George in Canada, then on to Vancouver and Seattle. In the other direction there is a plan to carve a 55-mile tunnel under the Bering Strait, linking fast bullet trains from New York to Beijing, Moscow, and London.

Compare such progress with a diary written by a one-room schoolhouse teacher with grades one through six at the beginning of the 20th century:

"At the end of this cold winter day, a heavy snow fell as I headed to the farm family where I boarded. It was a driving snow. Soon the mare plunged and foundered and seemed to get deeper and deeper in. I thought I would freeze to death in that drift. A farmer friend lived just up the road, and he was in the lot caring for his stock. He saw me and came with a shovel, unhitched the mare, and took us to his home for the night.

Playground equipment at the school was unheard of, but we didn't miss it. There were so many nice games to play. Blackman, dare-base, tug-of-war, crack-the-whip, hide-and-seek, kickthe wicket, jump rope and many more. I don't think we appreciated the great open spaces ahead."

The Duke University Center for Demographic Studies reports that with improving health, it is conceivable in the next few decades for someone to reach 130 years of age, beating the verified record of 122. In late life, to avoid wheeling around a renewing oxygen tank, we can all have a huge fresh oxygen tank overhead in the sky. Breathing in fresh air improves the circulation of blood into the vital organs of the heart and lungs. We can add exercise and eating from the top ten foods: tomatoes, olive oil, red grapes, nuts, whole grains, salmon, blueberries, spinach, and black or green tea. We can do much to entertain ourselves, alone or with others. We can watch or participate in sports and games, gardening, singing, sharing ideas, and reading. Ronald B. Shwartz in *For the Love of Books* has 115 celebrated authors discuss books they love. All kinds of activities can invigorate our health 60 to 120. 70,000 Americans are now crossing the century mark. The projection is for 800,000 in the near future.

Robert Frost wrote:

> *Two roads diverged in a wood, and I —*
> *I took the one less traveled by,*
> *And that has made all the difference*

Chapter Two

CREATIVITY

"In creating, the only hard thing's to begin." − James Russell Lowell

Introduction

Creativity Checklists

Brainstorming Ideas with Others

Journal Writing, Autobiography, and Letter Writing

Writing Simple Poetry

Amateur Art: Painting, Drawing, Cartooning

Collecting: Making Photography, Picture, or Other Scrapbooks

Brain Teasers for Creativity

Gardening Excitement

Exploring with the Internet and E Mail

Becoming an Independent Scholar

INTRODUCTION

The challenge and delight of becoming older is discovering new time for creativity. We can be free to chase our dreams and make our future. Physical power may decline; the curve for wisdom can go up. If we play up our strengths, people do not notice our aging. The further plus to aging is that leisure takes over where work existed — a new frontier.

The excitement of learning never ceases as long as we have breath. To massage an idea, we read about the subject and maybe include some training. It is called the scientific method — a problem is defined, a possible solution advanced, and a prediction is made. Related data is collected, tested, and conclusions are drawn. If it does not work out, we return to the drawing board, willing to try another tack. With patience and adjustments, we are likely to find a winner. Creativity can be as simple as committing a thought to paper. We continue to live like champions, a decade at a time, validating life.

Creativity is a constant challenge in the interplay of ideas. Renewal comes from inspiration, in consummating a performance, and relaxing to enjoy it. In later life one can set his own pace with no one looking over his shoulder. One is free of pressures and responsibilities with a lot of good years ahead. Women, of course, have the statistical advantage of living six years longer than men, extending the opportunity to stay engaged and to enjoy new experiences. Most women never retire from doing some laundry, cleaning, and meal preparation; but new time is found to explore spiritual beliefs, to join study groups, to attend museum and library programs, to do a little traveling, and to donate service time. Some people move to a warmer climate. Others choose a college town where they see a lot of young faces. Many prefer the familiarity of their homestead and in very late life move to a nearby first class retirement home with a broad offering of activities and continued learning.

With aging we become experts at using time, a precious commodity that everyone shares equally. We should not fritter away such a valuable asset. We no longer waste time reading "mush" or listening to "talking heads" on television. We can now find daily time for a rewarding project or two. For repeated renewal of our energy, we now have time to walk in the neighborhood or afield to refresh the lungs with oxygen and release the mind for reflections.

We can now explore new options. Each waking hour is a unique time that never was and never will be available again. One is free at last to explore the treasure chest of ideas and hunches that lie hidden in the brain. Discovering any solution is creative — it may be as simple as making a new acquaintance with whom to share ideas and to receive back new knowledge and experience.

Options and opportunities abound. Verdi composed operatic masterpieces at 80. Marilla Salisbury walked just under 5 miles an hour at age 80. Anna Mary Robertson Moses (Grandma Moses) didn't discover she could paint until after age 60. She had her first one-woman show when she was 80 and continued painting until 101. Marion Hart made seven solo flights across the Atlantic, the last time when she was 80.

New ideas and inspiration can be garnered from newspapers, magazines, books, television, radio, and even advertisements.

Everyone has innate talents to speak and write and to set goals. We draw from our bank of experiences. Often we do something creative during the day without recognizing it. We can manipulate our collected knowledge into new combinations. Carrying a small pocket pad to record flashes of intuition that may otherwise be lost is helpful.

Developing the art of conversation can be creative in discovering what others have experienced. Another option that we can develop is creative travel down memory lane with an edited scrapbook of favorite photos, adding published photos from magazines that bring back memories. These can be added to throughout life and reviewed in the comfort of an easy chair when there are no television programs or other activities at the moment to stir our imagination.

Some do creative ceramics for their own soul. At age 86 Vito Abate of Ann Arbor, Michigan has applied for admission to the University's prestigious music school, confident about his voice and wanting to push it to be better. When asked why he is choosing to matriculate, his reply is, "to dream the impossible dream."

Some break the monotony of the middle of the week with round robin get-togethers, with members providing parts of a meal or in making do without a meal. A creative party is enough!

Don't get discouraged. Carl Sandburg, the Chicago prairie poet, was unflappable in the face of setbacks. Needless to say, he had a poem for it:

There's no harm in trying,
Nothing can harm you till it comes
And it may never come
Or if it comes it is something else again.

And those who say, "I'll try anything once,"
Often try nothing twice, three times,
Arriving late at the gate of dreams worth dying for.

A first-rate soup is better than a fourth-rate painting. Or one can work with the most complex medium of all — people. One has only to evoke the child within oneself to seek something new, something authentic, and gets satisfaction from doing it. We can further our private education by studying great teachers: Jesus, Buddha, R.W. Emerson, John Dewey, Joseph Campbell, Oliver Wendell Holmes, William James, Alfred Lloyd Whitehead, or Colette, for example.

A temporary setback or failure is not confused with self-worth. Dr. Jonas Salk, discoverer of the polio vaccine, said, "I personally don't think in terms of disappointments and failures. I learn from all experiences, whether they come out positively or negatively. One goes forward with failure. If one makes a mistake or must compromise, and all do, one creates a problem. A problem often has a spin-off of a new insight and opportunity if one makes clever use of it." A weakness may well become a source of strength as blindness and deafness were for Helen Keller. An historic example of creative compromise was Goethe, living in a medieval town in Germany. He developed a consuming but impossible dream, "Ich vill die ganze welt verstehen — I will the whole world understand." Though he never reached his goal he kept learning throughout his life and in the process became a loved playwright and poet. Philosopher Neitzche said, "Do things you want to do — follow your bliss. Energy comes from doing what we want to do and excelling in it."

CREATIVITY CHECKLISTS

Write down what first comes to mind:

The future is_____

An ideal activity is_____

I want to know_____

I look forward to_____

I am best_____

I need_____

The happiest times are_____

I dream of_____

Some ideas to get started:

    Start or join a reading group and exchange books

    Do crafts, arts, photography, creative cooking

    Brainstorm ideas and become an independent scholar

    Become a story teller, do book reviews

    Be a political activist

    Join a current events club

    Join a genealogical group

    Organize games and coach

    Become a community volunteer

    Rent movie classics

    Become a movie and television critic

    Become an amateur astronomer or other science specialist, such as a meteorologist

    Keep an active bird sighting or tree sighting list

    Improve sleeping habits (1/3 of our lives)

Visit museums and libraries

Play an instrument

Become a gardener, indoor or outdoor

Attend adult education classes

Sing and dance

Become a volunteer teacher's aide or a special tutor

Become a reader of encyclopedias — a generalist or
a specialist

Prepare and lecture on state, national, or world wonders

Lead tours — local or area places of special interest

Become a consumer activist

Become an investment planner

Write Letters to the Editor

For self-analysis, compare yourself to the total population by indicating where you think you would fall in the pursuit of creativity, 50 being average, 25 below average, and 75 above average. The dots give opportunity to select one of the point intervals from 1 to 99.

	Percentile										
	1	10	20	30	40	50	60	70	80	90	99
Mechanical Interest	·	·	·	·	·	·	·	·	·	·	·
Communicative Skills	·	·	·	·	·	·	·	·	·	·	·
Listening Skills	·	·	·	·	·	·	·	·	·	·	·
Understanding People											
Computational Skills	·	·	·	·	·	·	·	·	·	·	·
Use of Creativity	·	·	·	·	·	·	·	·	·	·	·
Persuasiveness	·	·	·	·	·	·	·	·	·	·	·
Clerical Interest	·	·	·	·	·	·	·	·	·	·	·
Understands Self	·	·	·	·	·	·	·	·	·	·	·
Scientific Interest	·	·	·	·	·	·	·	·	·	·	·
Concerns for Others											
and Social Service	·	·	·	·	·	·	·	·	·	·	·
Time Management Skills	·	·	·	·	·	·	·	·	·	·	·
Literary Interest	·	·	·	·	·	·	·	·	·	·	·
Self-Discipline	·	·	·	·	·	·	·	·	·	·	·
Problem Solving Ability	·	·	·	·	·	·	·	·	·	·	·
Musical Appreciation	·	·	·	·	·	·	·	·	·	·	·
Social Skills	·	·	·	·	·	·	·	·	·	·	·
Aesthetic Artistic Interest	·	·	·	·	·	·	·	·	·	·	·
Speaking Ability Before											
Others	·	·	·	·	·	·	·	·	·	·	·
Optimistic Attitude	·	·	·	·	·	·	·	·	·	·	·
Ability to Work with											
Others	·	·	·	·	·	·	·	·	·	·	·
Decision-making Skill	·	·	·	·	·	·	·	·	·	·	·
Energy Level	·	·	·	·	·	·	·	·	·	·	·
Enthusiasm	·	·	·	·	·	·	·	·	·	·	·
Self-Confidence	·	·	·	·	·	·	·	·	·	·	·
Emotional Control	·	·	·	·	·	·	·	·	·	·	·

BRAINSTORMING IDEAS WITH OTHERS

Whether thinking through a problem alone or interacting with others, many methods of thinking and kinds of intelligence are used. Convergent and divergent thinking apply. One narrows an idea down after exploding in all directions for discovery. A guideline for any problem is to try to simplify it, not complicate it. One approach is to turn the problem upside down and see what happens. Reverse or inverse thinking may come to the rescue. Goals are reached by cut-and-try, by sleeping on the problem, by alterations, and by setting a deadline. If the deadline is not reached, one lets go and starts on something else.

Creativity can be simple and is present in all of us. Pick up some small-sized pebbles and toss them straight up. If there is a wind, they fall to one side. Measure the sidewise drift and one has a wind gauge.

The number of different types of intelligence makes a long list that is growing:

- Constructive thinking related to common sense
- Interpersonal skill in reading another's feelings
- Street smarts often exhibited by minorities
- High level creativity, a rare commodity
- Judgment and insight in putting facts together
- Executive process ability to plan, motivate, and evaluate
- Practical intelligence in exercising tricks of a trade
- Goal oriented intelligence to perform long term projects
- Artistic talent in music, art, creative writing
- Kinesthetic intelligence demonstrated by athletes and dancers

- Drive and perserverance intelligence
- Ethical intelligence
- Social intelligence — listener, friend, mediator
- Love and trust intelligence
- Wisdom intelligence gained over a lifetime

The mind receives thousands of impressions or stimuli each day. The whole business of being alive has so many demands that one needs short-term memory as well as long-term to reduce traffic in the brain. As one ages, one slows down, savors long-term memories, and enjoys the immediate surroundings. More and more women are discovering that they are creative. Now emancipated, they are becoming politicians, scientists in laboratories, business leaders, and entering all other fields of endeavor. Women are more people-oriented than men are; they may become better politicians. The country will welcome them.

Brainstorming has a few basic rules:

1. Criticism is ruled out; judgment is deferred
2. Free-wheeling is welcomed; the wilder or more unusual the idea the better
3. Quantity is desired — the greater the number of ideas the greater the results
4. Combination and improvement of the ideas are sought; one listens and hitchhikes on other's ideas
5. The object is to break out of ruts and jump into wider worlds to get a stronger punch
6. The dream must be big and simple
7. Develop something that is needed by society and that can be continually improved.

By advancing in the direction of a dream, we then live the life imagined. We become patient for life to throw the right curve that we can lean into. It may require the patience of Job. Think of Nelson Mandela, who endured prison for 26 years before becoming the leader of his country, South Africa. In prison he focused on goals and never gave up. Each person has the potential to make a contribution, great or small.

We live in a period of rapid change; new windows are opened almost daily. Life is a plethora of choices. We should create a short list of achievable projects and start with the easiest ones. Ever more technology in the new century feeds creativity offering more opportunity than the industrial revolution of the century just passed.

One way to get started is to have a desk calendar and decide upon a simple objective for the morning and another for the afternoon. In the evening there can be a few moments of evaluation, striking off an achievement and revising the list for another day. In the business of life, take regular inventory and make revisions. Women are always doing; men can copy that.

Brainstorming is not reserved for academics. Often discoveries are made by lab assistants and ordinary citizens exploring a hunch. We can all become independent scholars pursuing a creative idea. An example of a creative choice was Hal Holbrook doing performances as Mark Twain. The author did the same with Carl Sandburg, reading his poems of the people and excerpts from Sandburg's seminal six volumes on Abraham Lincoln, which claimed Lincoln to be the greatest person in American history.

Exchanging ideas with others helps in picking a project. We

learn to let go and let the imagination soar. In retirement people are free to be artists in language, in song, in art, in dance — weaving life into a creative web. Discoveries never cease as long as we keep experimenting with materials and new pathways. Everyone has foresight at odd moments. Clarence Darrow, the lawyer, thought up the game of Monopoly in such a moment. Start social interaction with others of like interests, i.e. a reading club for enlightenment and entertainment. Consider writing a life story or a family history as a contribution to the science of genealogy and gerontology. If necessary, collaborate with a biographer. The local historical society will welcome the manuscript for succeeding generations.

Throughout history thinkers have recognized the need for liberating the self.

"The unexamined life is not worth living."
Socrates
"Anything we think of and believe we can achieve."
William James
"Success is to grasp the situation, to adapt oneself to it, and to exploit it to one's own advantage."
Charles de Gaulle

JOURNAL WRITING, AUTOBIOGRAPHY, AND LETTER WRITING

For creativity if one has never written, now is the time to start. Writing down reflections about events experienced each day is called journal writing. It is not a diary but a container of reflections. It contains self-expressions and self-exploration — thoughts, feelings, and concerns as well. Emotions can be expressed in the privacy of the page. Needs and goals are easier to clarify when recorded. One is thus better able to understand oneself and other people.

Journal writing acts as a self-adjusting compass in creative freedom. Ideas become easier to prioritize when written down. One may set aside twenty minutes each evening, take some deep breaths, and focus one's attention inward. It is as simple as jotting down a few lines to summarize the high and low points of the day.

Journal writing is for daily or weekly recording, however brief, of daily and weekly events, contacts, and news. Many have done this annually in a Christmas letter. In such writing one can highlight one's life and better develop possibilities for one's future. When the creative person unfolds, one can often form new directions and goals.

Journal writing is a good use of one's time. No prior experience is needed. One just starts writing. It is how we create ourselves in memory for the people, places, objects, events, and feelings that go on each day. It becomes our life story or the life story of a loved one, his dreams and sacrifices, to give a lifetime perspective, a whole or in part.

Anne Frank, in Holland, hiding from the Nazi storm troopers hunting down Jews, found comfort in writing a diary. At age 15 she was uncovered and exterminated in a Nazi gas chamber. Her childhood memories have lived on, becoming classic history and literature.

Autobiographies have been a central source in recorded history. Women have been and increasingly are contributing to writing. They live longer and are not as reticent as men.

There is a unique autobiography in everyone. "I sit in my easy chair at 85. There is the sound of traffic in the distance. It never ceases, 24 hours a day, so close is the expressway. Where is everyone going at over 70 miles per hour?" One looks back in memory: 85 years ago on Saturday Father hitched old Molly to the buggy for the seven mile ride to the county seat to sell door-to-door fruits and vegetables grown on the farm. The next day the family of seven grouped to attend Sunday school and church two miles away after fording a stream. In the afternoon one stayed at home to receive neighbors or went visiting depending upon arrangements made at church. Adding this memory to my journal has been rewarding. In journal writing the hand moves almost automatically. It might even produce a wake-up call to become a better steward of one's life. It becomes inexpensive therapy. In remembering the fun of the past, one can uncover what is fun for the future.

Tomorrow I may write a Letter to the Editor of our local newspaper — another method of self-exploration and expression. The satisfaction of writing letters is a universal language. One can add creativity by outlining one's autobiography, memories, and future visions, including achievements, great loves, closest friends, favorite past times. Or it might be easier to talk into a tape recorder. The main thing is to set aside some time each day for such an exercise. One becomes a hero of one's own life story.

Writing classes with a leader are available in senior centers and adult education classes, or one can start one's own neighborhood writing group. In increasing numbers people are joining to write and tell stories — their own.

Everyone has a story to tell. Others have written Appalachian hill stories, stories of conquering the West, comments on the conflicts of our times and of inventions that have changed our lives, stories of great wars in our history, stories about our great leaders, book reviews, and poems. To enthrall children read to them Sidney Lanier's "Song of the Chattahooche". To enthrall elders read to them of the perserverance evidenced in Stephen Vincent Benet's "Ballad of William Sycamore". People are interested in experiences we have had as a child, in school, and in adult life.

Sharing experiences can be fun. We can walk the Appalachian Trail without stepping foot on it by enjoying Bill Bryson's book *A Walk in the Woods*. It is full of the author's and a friend's hilarious adventures as they covered the 2,100 miles from Georgia to Maine. There are acute observations too on the magnificence of this area with a plea for its preservation.

Composing a heartfelt letter or note to a friend is being creative. Creativity produces psychological health. For personal satisfaction and for sharing, one can create an album of family photographs and favorite photos from throwaway magazines. On a lonely or cold winter night such an album can furnish a warming glow. Creativity can be as simple as an innovation in the kitchen or an afternoon stroll leading to contemplation. What one thinks, feels, and does is then shared with others.

Recent Books on Creative Writing:

How to Write Your Own Life Story by Lois Daniels
This Is Your Life Story by Velma Krauch
Families Writing by Peter Stillman
The New Diary by Tristine Raineer
Wild Mind by Natalie Goldberg
Writing Down the Bones by Natalie Goldberg
Journal to the Self by Kathleen Adams
Writing for Your Life by Diana Metzger
Journey Notes by Richard Solly
Focus on the Positive by Peter McWilliams
At a Journal Workshop by Ira Progoff

A LIST OF WRITING IDEAS

{Compiled from many sources including Lois Daniels' *How to Write Your Own Life Story* and Velma Krauch's *This Is Your Life Story*.}

1. Your first memories, "secret gardens"
2. House you lived in as a child, your neighborhood
3. Toys, games you played
4. Clothing you wore as a child
5. Pets
6. What summer meant to you (winter, spring, fall)
7. A favorite snapshot
8. Your family: mother, father, sisters, brothers
9. Your grandparents, other relatives
10. Pals, friends (by school grades or ages of life or locations)
11. Early school years, favorite subjects, teachers
12. Birthdays
13. Adolescence
14. Illnesses and remedies
15. Religious training
16. Places your family lived
17. Early jobs you had
18. Holidays: Christmas, etc.
19. Instruments you played
20. High school, dreams of the future you had
21. Relations with the other sex, dating
22. Family vacations, family traditions, stories
23. Leaving home for the first time

24. College, teachers, social life, adventures
25. Historical events, e.g. wars, Depression, world history
26. First real job
27. Courtship/wedding (if applicable)
28. Husband or wife
29. Married years
30. Your career life
31. Birth of first child, raising a family
32. Divorce (if applicable)
33. When children left home
34. Weddings of children, in-laws
35. Grandchildren
36. Life as a widow/widower (if applicable)
37. Retirement years
38. "If I had my life to live over, I would…."
39. "As I look ahead, I plan to…."
40. A happy period in your life, a difficult period
41. Turning points in your life
42. Your worst mistake, your smartest decision
43. An accomplishment of which you are most proud
44. Your involvement with the community
45. Unusual trip, adventure, vacation
46. Hobbies and leisure interests
47. Family recipes
48. Artifacts, keepsakes, heirlooms
49. Values and ideals from your parents

WRITING SIMPLE POETRY

Gwen Frostic, weighing less than 100 pounds at age 94, lives alone with her companion fox terrier, Elliott, on her 40 acres of wild woods along the Betsie River in northern Michigan. Benzonia is the nearest town. Here she preserves nature in writing and with block prints art. A mysterious illness during infancy left her with physical aftereffects similar to cerebral palsy. She had her house built with raw fieldstones and a sod roof. Walls are sliced logs with bark side up. Branches became handrails, driftwood became doorknobs. The outdoor landscaping is all natural. She lives above her shop and twice a day feeds the creatures of the woods from her porch. If she is by herself at Christmas time, that's fine. She is happy and she knows it.

Over the past 26 years in her basement, eighteen Heidelberg presses have clanked out block prints to illustrate her poetry about the natural world, ringing up sales to make her a millionaire. In the retail shop on the main floor cats sleep on the counters, squirrel tracks mark the floor, and a natural well gurgles.

Intrigued by Frostic and her creativity, the author searched her early writing for samples of her poetry when she was more ambulatory and taking walks on the sand dunes overlooking Lake Michigan:

> *Upon the edge of the bluffs*
> *   look far out on the waves —*
> *Out where the sky begins*
> *   and white clouds form.*

Soon a gull drifts by in the wind and little
sandpipers appear on the beach below –
and you are not alone.

A later poem:

In the open fields
where sweet clover blows
and Queen Anne's lace and asters grow,
a bumblebee hums among the flowers
and little goldfinches fill the air –
and your are not alone.
All seems so still –
leaves rustle a bit and a chipmunk runs –
a little toad sits on deep green moss –
and you are not alone.

Each day is a miracle
that you come to know –
how much a part of everything you are –
how much all things
are part of you –
and you are not alone.

The power to enjoy and write poetry is universal. The Poet Laureate of the United States, Robert Pinsky, says, "There is something mystical in poetry. It is a combination of an intellectual, metaphysical, and emotional experience. People in ordinary workaday settings can partake of that experience."

To write amateur poetry one writes about the simple sounds, sights, and smells one enjoys. By exercising one's imagination one can become a millionaire in ideas, much more exciting than money. One may have said, " I am not much of a cook" and then becomes one. With a small hand lens one can discover nature's marvelous secrets hidden from normal sight. Seeing the small can make one more aware of the larger world. Observation, aided by research to increase word choice, can lead to expression in simple poetic form. Small things can grow large when written by a darer, a learner, and a doer. Writing talent is thus uncovered or rediscovered.

Beginning writers often enjoy the Haiku poetic form. The HAIKU is a traditional Japanese verse form of seventeen syllables, most often expressing the poet's emotion and/or insight into seasonal or natural phenomena. These verbal snapshots usually appear in three lines, having five, seven, and then five syllables.

Example:

> *Tea water, tired*
> *waiting while we watched the snow....*
> *froze itself a hat.*
>
> Sokan, Japanese

If we can count syllables and observe nature, we can feel triumph and exhilaration, becoming a tamer of words. The following were done by an amateur senior Haiku group.

SPRING

Early spring willows
swirling their supple branches
in golden cascade.

Thousands of trillium
mask the forest floor.
Hyperbole — yes!

SUMMER

Along the pond's path,
lilac scent and massed color
silently shout: STOP!

So fragile, tasteful —
red raspberries for breakfast.
A peach too. I'm blest.

FALL

Silent circling hawk
writes in air with delicate
sky calligraphy.

Constellation-pierced
midnight sky's embroidered robe
covers sleeping earth.

WINTER

The wind swirls new snow
like ever-shifting lawn dunes.
Is that hill wave-made?

Branches snow-laden creak
and snap in whistling winds —
winter concerto.

AMATEUR ART: PAINTING, DRAWING, CARTOONING

Anyone who can push a pencil can draw stick figures. A stick figure can be embellished to illustrate an event or make an observation. A cartoon is born!

Artists and philosophers, many of whom are productive into their nineties, start by violating a sheet of paper with a line or thought. The artist Picasso started a new work with a simple line. Finding regular times to sit down alone and concentrate on recording ideas is half the battle in planning. Often the clue to a new outlet is a lateral move or an expansion of a previously enjoyed activity.

Simple drawings or just combinations of color made by chalk or crayons become amateur art. There is some artistic talent in everyone. Moving to watercolors, one can attempt a reproduction of a picture found on a calendar or in a magazine. One can construct art of ordinary materials. The art of collage is interesting: arranging bits of pictures, figures, letters, or words on a theme to make a designed or artistic whole. The really ambitious might advance to painting with oils.

In late life there is time to explore new goals. In such a search flexibility and getting assistance by learning from others will lead to a more creative life. We will be doing things we didn't think that we could do. Bill Traylor, a folk art painter, did not pick up a paintbrush until he was 85 years old. William Edmunson, the first black to have a solo exhibit in the New York Museum of Modern Art, was in his middle 60s when the hospital where he was a janitor closed, and he began his first experience with art.

Those who want to design useful objects may turn out to be inventors or late life explorers. Who knows where design and use of simple materials might lead? The accumulation of experience and knowledge is a valuable bank to draw from. An example of how a hobby can change the world occurred in the late 1920s. A tiny, single-engined crate overloaded with gasoline barely rose from a Long Island, New York airfield with the barest essentials — a small rubber raft, a knife, some flares, watches, fishing equipment, and five thin sandwiches — no radio, no sextant. At times for good air, flying ten feet above the sea with spray covering the windshield, at other times at 10,000 feet above the clouds to avoid storms, 33 hours later Charles Lindbergh touched down in Paris. At that instant the world became a much smaller place and would never be the same. In the not too distant future, one will be able to fly anywhere in the world in two hours, rising to the stratosphere where there is no air resistance. Chances for peace will certainly increase when we all become such close neighbors.

COLLECTING: MAKING PHOTOGRAPHY, PICTURE, OR OTHER SCRAPBOOKS

One can create "pop art" by collecting family photos over the years and cutting out appealing pictures of natural or historic places seen or not seen from cast-off magazines. We can make a montage of clipped pictures with a common theme. Adding to and reviewing such favorite pictures is creative and relaxing. Stamp collections, coin collections, and matchbook collections are other collectibles that can also be an educationally challenging and entertaining hobby. For fun we can get out the albums to remember and enjoy them again and again.

Scrapbook and craft get-togethers are like sewing circles were in previous times. We swap ideas and learn from each other, often leading to sharing other stories to supply entertaining conversation and bonding.

Scrapbooks are about family, favorite scenes visited or collected from illustrations or expert photography from magazines, and best of all a record of photographs of one's own precious experiences. Scrapbooks can lead to a hobby of further genealogical research, which now has modern tools for assistance.

BRAIN TEASERS FOR CREATIVITY

Four rectangular cards of identical size are arranged as shown below. Form a square by moving only <u>one</u> card.

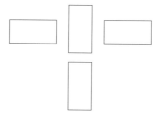

Draw this envelope with one continuous pencil line . . . but, you can't cross any lines to complete it!

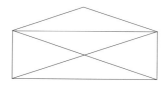

How many squares do you see?

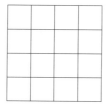

The triangle formed below has ten pennies and the point of the triangle is facing away from you. Move <u>only three</u> pennies to reverse the triangle so that it points towards you.

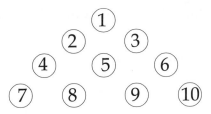

Six quarters firm two rows, one with three quarters, one with four. <u>Move one</u> coin to make two rows, <u>each</u> having <u>four</u> quarters.

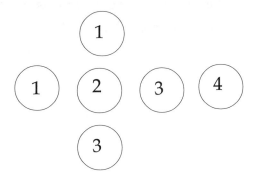

Twelve matches are placed on the table as shown below. Remove two matches and leave only two squares.

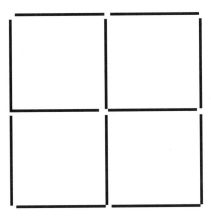

GARDENING EXCITEMENT

Gardening is creative. Flowers make perfectly realized figures of compelling beauty. It is said that there is a bulb for every situation and season and always a delight when it flowers. This can happen on a sunny indoor window ledge, the dining room table in January, or in a small plot outdoors in season. You can get bulbs to bloom whenever you want. There need to be drainage holes or bulbs will otherwise waterlog. Placing the pot inside another solves that problem. The approximate number of bulbs in a six-inch pot is eight to fifteen crocuses, three hyacinths, five iris danfordiae, up to ten iris reticulata, six narcissus, or four to five tulips. Bulbs are planted close together but not touching, can be stored and watered in a cool space for twelve weeks before being put on a sunny windowsill.

While most bulbs require months of dormancy, there are a couple of warm weather bulbs that can be planted any time and have an array of flowers in a matter of weeks — amaryllis and tazettas, such as the paper white narcissus.

If there is space for an outdoor garden, tomatoes, cucumbers, green beans, zucchini, and butternut squash can be grown. If there is room for flowers, make a perennial garden, a rose garden or plant pansies or impatiens around tree trunks. Adding a small garden at one's door or having plants on one's windowsill can become gardens of Eden, "a little world made cunningly", according to Emily Dickinson, who never left home.

Even the handicapped can find a New World with creative gardening:

One can do it in a window ledge garden.
One can do it in a small raised plot outdoors.
One can attach a small miniature greenhouse
      for year round use.

A small garden needs a plan, watering and weeding, sunlight, and the gift of good soil. It begins to sound like the ingredients for a person's flowering into late life, 60 to 100+.

The vision, smell, and touch of tending a garden are a primordial experience. Tending a garden is often more play than work; it is a love affair to some. It is pleasant to dig in the dirt, to transplant seedlings so that they may prosper. Even weeding brings a feeling of accomplishment — the garden is warding off invasion and conquest. As one feels the soil, he is at home in his own patch of earth.

Gardening truly treats the senses. Visiting others' formal or informal gardens, one replenishes the soul with their colors and arrangements. The fragrances make one at home in the world. Vegetables have freshness, zest, and tang; they are a treat to the palate. One sees different shades of green and yellow, the red of a watermelon slice, the ornamental quality of grapes with flavors ranging from sweet to tart. Then at the end of the growing season orange pumpkins are ready to become jack-o'-lanterns. Nurturing the growth of plants nurtures the self, fostering great satisfaction.

EXPLORING WITH THE INTERNET AND E-MAIL

The Internet may have the impact that radio and television had on the century just passed. Computers are becoming less expensive and thus available to more and more people. Senior centers and libraries have them available for public use. They can change the way we communicate, invest, learn, and the way we buy things.

In early times education was the privilege of the very rich, usually the young rich. Now lifelong learning with the world as our textbook becomes the prescription for late age. Education can be reconstructed to take place over the entire life span. Computers replace old textbooks. Educators share their knowledge worldwide. Exploring with the Internet and E-mail, one can surf for any information desired. No longer is anyone without an outlet for creativity and fulfillment.

Minorities can use the Internet as a great equalizer; every citizen has power at his fingertips. Click one's mouse and one gets facts, figures, pictures, graphs, or catalogs for ordering almost any item. Laptops can now do these functions with the convenience of mobility. Others cannot peek in on our activities since information is transmitted on a frequency only our receiver knows, even though millions of web sites are in existence.

The New York Times, found in almost every library as the newspaper of record, now has a special section each Thursday entitled "Circuits". Already continuing education is moving to the Internet for on-line instruction with regular faculty teaching the courses, such as how to live in the new century. The Internet can reach a person who has just climbed Mt. Everest!

The Internet can be used to explore literature, art, news, places of interest, and to make new friends. From our arm chairs we can communicate instantly with our acquaintances or organizations.

Most people with a few hour-long sessions can acquire computer knowledge. Classes are being offered in public libraries and community colleges. Some key strokes and mouse clicks, and you are in the computer age. Soon there may be palmheld phone/computers operated from our easy chairs. Web sites have been designed for the needs of the elderly, such as elder law, Medicare/Medicaid, estate planning, and the rights of the elderly.

New media, such as E-mail, will cannibalize older media, giving the advantage to those who have computers. Imagine a place open around the clock, seven days a week, where we can talk to medical experts, discover the latest arthritic treatments, or simply find a sympathetic ear. There can be discussion groups on chosen issues. Now programs can attach interactive game boards, so that people can play card, chess, and other games. Using these media and limiting their intrusion on our time becomes a game, or maybe even a problem for some.

One warning is for grandchildren. They take the mouse in hand as early as age four to explore a portal of games and toys. Children under age seven cannot distinguish between advertising and content. Free prizes for personal information is a no-no. Advertisers covet the youth market and the $130 billion buying power it represents. Even pornography is available to our youth. The hidden price of open accessibility is the invasion of privacy, questions of security, and reliability. The revenue from advertising is the gimmick. Staying safe on-line is in knowing what to say and what to avoid.

What is productive for adults may not be productive for children. Grandparents can know what grandchildren are seeing on the Internet while their parents are working. At-home women, children, and minorities now have access to the world. While relatives are traveling, they can share their experiences with those who stayed at home. The latter can travel vicariously the adventures of others. Even school classes follow the travels and experiences of others.

With this new arrival on the world scene, information is transmitted with instantaneous speed. We can listen while doing other things, unlike print media, that require total attention. The great advantage is that we can interact immediately to share our opinion. Someone might respond with an addition or correction. We have established a contact with a total stranger; we may want to develop further contacts to create an exchange.

We might introduce a book, a literary figure, or a prominent news story for reaction and discussion. Others might pick it up and join in. We might study a foreign language, book tickets to a cultural or sporting event, buy airline tickets, or do all kinds of research. There are E-mail discussion lists, bulletin boards, and news groups with announced topics and themes. We can choose to float in and out of conversations.

This new medium has the ability to elevate and expand public discourse. It is growing faster than any other in economic history. If it has problems, it also can provide solutions. The potential for global electronic commerce is enhanced by the Internet, but government action may be necessary to protect consumers. To repeat, privacy becomes a question. The number one issue on the minds of surfers is trust. Get rich schemes and pornography are issues as well as pseudo-journalism. One has to be careful to whom one gives financial or other private information. (Pornography content is not new — it is found on television, at local video stores, and at movie theaters.)

But the advantages persist: the free flow of information across national borders and the offering of more affordable products and services to a global audience. Web sites allow television quality videos for businesses to deliver information and products with an instant showroom. Net sites are now selling cars directly, bypassing the dealer. For a monthly fee, by dialing a toll-free number, we can already retrieve our E-mail messages if we are away from home. The day is not far away when we will be able to get on any computer to get a text readout of our voice mail when away from home. We may be in only the second inning of a nine inning ball game.

BECOMING AN INDEPENDENT SCHOLAR

Charles Kuralt at 60+ freed himself from regular responsibilities in television, looked ahead, and "saw the road was bending". What could be around the bend? He bought a camper and took off. Every turn of the road became unique, a new discovery in sight.

Psychologist William James wrote that persons of creativity arise from ordinary people with aims and purposes on which they concentrate. Karen Horney says everyone has the capacity to change and grow as long as he lives. Henry David Thoreau said, "of over four billion people on earth, no two are alike, and none will be like me again. Whatever we can do or dream about doing, beginning it has power and magic in it."

There is a scholar in everyone. All we need for a start is to explore a topic that intrigues us. We can do holiday and travel planning to suit our taste. We can become our own weather observer, forecaster, and analyst. After studying cookbooks, newspapers, or television we can cook. Some even cook without a cookbook!

We can use libraries in our neighborhood to explore ideas. There are often "Learning in Retirement" programs in our locality. With C-Span there are book reviews to stir the imagination. We can develop a talk about a book recently read. We can write letters to the editor to reach a wide audience.

A remarkable example is Jessie Foveaux, who at age 98 sold her memoir *Any Given Day* for one million dollars after taking a writing class for seniors in Manhattan, Kansas. She flew for the first time, appeared on New York talk shows, and was written about in newspapers for publicity purposes. She took in all the hoopla matter-of-factly, as she had other events in her long, often difficult, life.

Life can offer too many distractions. Sometimes it is wise to lie down on the ground, smell the air, or look at the sky through the trees; then just maybe inspiration will come. Communing with ourselves becomes a fine art. We need never stop experimenting with a new idea.

Chapter Three

FUN FUNCTION-- RENEWAL

If a person insisted on being serious and never allowed a bit of fun one would become old without knowing it—Herodotus 484 BC, Father of History

Laughing All the Way

Nature: It's There, It's Free, Enjoy It!

Travel: Pleasure Via Donkey or Sea Freighter!

Pleasures of Reading

Stories and Jokes

Dancing for Wallflowers: Square, Single, or Line

Singing and Listening to Old and New Songs

Films: Meet Me in the Balcony for a Great Matinee or on the Couch for a Classic Rental!

Fun and Games: Wherever You Are, Indoors or Out

The Actor in You: Role Playing or Group Pantomime with a Reader

Redefining Sex for Fun

Our Best Friends: Pets -- Real or Non-Real at One's Feet

LAUGHING ALL THE WAY

Fun function is an expression of freedom outside the realm of "should" or "must", perhaps a taste of utopia and moments of paradise. If things can pass through one's prism, one has the best and cheapest health companion. Humor can diffuse firecracker moments eliminating the tenseness of an up-tight situation.

Norman Cousins in his book *Anatomy of an Illness* says that when he laughed, many healthy things occurred in his body. There was greater oxygen intake: blood pressure went down. Chemicals were released that were natural pain killers as tears of laughter contain an immune substance which fights viruses in the body.

One connects with others through laughter. Ashley Montagu, the anthropologist, says seeing the ludicrous and amusing in the somber adds flavor to living. He wants the elderly to cultivate the child in the self, to fly one's spirit like a kite -- to love, to laugh, to dance, to sing, to wonder, to play, to create, and to care for others. All these are health companions. Barbra Streisand sings, "People who like people are the luckiest people in the world."

Subjects to Share with Friends

Current politics

The weather

One's hopes and dreams

Embarrassments

Sports events

A current joke

One's youth

Historical heroes

Exchange of ideas

Favorite stories

Recent good books

Health news

The arts and music

Questions on whatever

Historical events

Shopping suggestions

Mutual friends

Accomplishments

Family, relatives

Failures

Predictions

Current heroes

Future plans

The best in television and radio

Dislikes

Why women live longer

Spiritual life

Investments

NATURE: IT'S THERE, IT'S FREE, ENJOY IT!

"A person in love with nature never grows old" is an old Turkish proverb. Arthur Miller, the American playwright, speaks of our watching the trees and the trees watching us. Life starts anew for all humankind with each sunrise. The animals change location at dawn. The day feeders are coming out in song and nocturnals are seeking shelter. Sit down and listen about 20 feet from a fence line as animals move along the sides. At dusk there is a reversal, the nocturnals are coming out and the day feeders are retiring with vesper song. At mid-morning, high noon, or mid-afternoon a world never known before can be opened by an inexpensive 10 power hand microscope carried on one's key chain. These microscopes can magnify the internal beauty of flowers and plants and observe insects that are everywhere. Have you seen a springtail flea dance in the snow? Field glasses or an arm telescope bring in startling details of beauty from the distance. The details of dawn, daylight shadows, and dusk can never be foreseen and will never be repeated in the same nuances.

Nature is free to everyone regardless of age and status, a never failing friend, and a source of fun and relaxation. One may not be able to follow Darwin to the Galapagos Islands, but everyone can escape to the landscape and skyscape at hand. In a city there are public parks and open spaces, even cemeteries in which one can relax to better note changes in the seasons, perhaps an animal at play, and a bird in flight.

Trees are fascinating offering six shapes — pyramidal, conical, columnar, spreading, vase-shaped, and rounded. They have nine clues to identification: height, age determined from diameter, leaves, bark, twigs, flowers, fruit, natural habitat, and range.

Plants in spring are hepatica, spring beauty, trillium (white or red), trout lily, marsh marigolds, may apple, anemone, and bloodroot.

Summer brings ragwort, wild carrot, Solomon's seal, goldenrod, sunflowers, and bloodroot.

For indoor pleasure the nearest library has books authored by great naturalists. To expand fun in nature, read books by John Muir, Loren Eiseley, Rene Dubos, John Burroughs, Enos Mills, Black Elk, Theodore Roosevelt, Gifford Pinchot, Aldo Leopold, Eliot Porter, Donald Peattie, Joseph Krutch, W. H. Hudson, and many others.

Nature is the subject of poems by Elizabeth Barrett Browning, William Cullen Bryant, Rupert Brooke, Robert Burns, Emily Dickinson, Ralph Waldo Emerson, Jean Ingelow, Sidney Lanier, Lucy Larcom, Henry Wadsworth Longfellow, James R. Lowell, Alfred Tennyson, Henry van Dyke, John G. Whittier, and Walt Whitman.

At any time a walk in the woods reacquaints the self with nature. Some plants whisper constantly. A strong wind can make them chatter. It is said that in the corn belt of the Midwest in the quiet of the night one can hear the corn grow. Its rustle in the slightest breeze never disappoints. In the fall deciduous trees furnish the pleasure of falling leaves. During daylight hours bird and animal sounds can form a symphony. Bees work endlessly during the day, and the sounds of crickets and grasshoppers fill the air. In season the katydids rap out their sexual song as do the cicadas from high in the trees.

In one's backyard or neighboring open space, seeds, acorns,

or one's own table scraps can be used to attract wildlife. Birds can be called with "pssh" sounds.

Plants to Attract Birds

Trees and Shrubs:

American Bittersweet	Beautyberry	Beech
Birch	Blackberry	Brambles
Blackgum	Blueberry	Buttonbush
Wild Cherry	Chokecherry	Elderberry
Crabapple	Dogwoods	Euonymus
Hawthorn	Hemlock	Holly
Huckleberry	Mulberry	Oak
Persimmon	Pines	American Plum
Red Cedar	Sassafras	Serviceberry
Spiceberry	Sumac	Tulip Tree

Perennials and Vines:

Asters	Bee Balm	Black-eyed Susan
Blazing Star	Bushclover	Butterflyweed
Cardinal Flower	Columbine	Coreopsis
Fire Pink	Goldenrods	Wild Grapes
Hibiscus family	Joe Pye Weed	Penstemon
Senna, wild	Spiderwort	Trumpet Honey
Honeysuckle	Virginia Creeper	Wild Bleeding Heart

Native Grasses:
Big Bluestem, Broomsedge, Bushy Beardgrass, Indian Grass, Little Bluestem, Switch Grass, Sidesoats Grama

A Starter Bird List
for the Eastern United States

Great blue heron

Green-backed heron

Canada goose

Mallard duck

Blue-winged teal

Wood duck

Turkey vulture

Cooper's hawk

American kestrel

Killdeer

Semipalmated sandpiper

Rock dove

Mourning dove

Hairy woodpecker

Downy woodpecker

Tree swallow

Bank swallow

Barn swallow

Purple martin

Blue jay

American crow

Black-capped chickadee

Yellow-throated vireo

Red-eyed vireo

Warbling vireo

Nashville warbler

Yellow warbler

Yellow-rumped warbler

Palm warbler

Common yellowthroat

Wilson's warbler

House sparrow

Eastern meadowlark

Red-winged blackbird

Northern oriole

Common grackle

Brown-headed cowbird

Scarlet tanager

Northern cardinal

Rose-breasted grosbeak

American goldfinch

Chipping sparrow

Field sparrow

Swamp sparrow

White-breasted nuthatch	Song sparrow
Tufted titmouse	House wren
Gray catbird	American robin
Blue-gray gnatcatcher	European starling

On vacations one can go farther afield for fun. In the East one can walk a part of the 2,100 mile Appalachian Trail that stretches from Springer Mountain in Georgia to Mt. Katahdin in Maine offering astonishing landscapes of silent forests and sparkling lakes. In one's favorite chair one can enjoy such a trek in Bill Bryon's book *A Walk in the Woods*, a great vicarious experience and funny too.

There are similar trails all over America. The North Country Trail starts near the top of New York State and winds over the top of the Midwest into North Dakota. The West is full of striking trails through mountains, by pure lakes and streams. Find tall pines and enter a cathedral. Find the music of cottonwood and aspen leaves dancing in the wind. Locate a nearby pool of water, pond, stream , or lake to enjoy the dazzling beauty of light transposed on the surface by the slow movement of the sun's light.

Helen Hayes, the actress, said all she had to do for fun was to step outside her door and things began to happen. Watching people is fascinating. They have unique walking styles and facial expressions that are clues to their personalities. No one need live in loneliness where nature and greeting people abound.

HENRY DAVID THOREAU
AS SEEN BY CONTEMPORARIES

In 1844 R.W. Emerson purchased land bordering on Walden Pond, not far from Concord, Massachusetts. Thoreau asked permission to live on the land and soon thereafter constructed a small hut for a total cost of $28.12. He moved into his new home on July 4, 1845 and lived there for over two years, until September 6, 1847. During that time he conducted what has become America's most famous experiment in simple living. Spending only 27 cents per week on necessities, Thoreau sought to simplify his life to the essentials and to find out what would happen.

His needs were kept to a minimum, so for hours and hours, day after day, Thoreau was faced with few demands on his time. The land was open for him to use as he saw fit. The activities with which most of us busy up our lives were not part of his days by Walden Pond. And so he was faced with the question of "What's left? When you wipe your days clean of what you usually do, what remains? When alone, without family, without friends, without obligations, what does one live for?"

One lives for the morning.

He wrote, "The morning, which is the most memorable season of the day, is the awakening hour. Then there is least (drowsiness) in us; and for an hour , at least, some part of us awakes which slumbers all the rest of the day and night... Morning is when I am awake and there is a dawn in me... To be awake is to be alive. I have never yet met a man who was completely awake. How could I have looked him in the face?"

One lives for sounds.

"The sound of crickets at dawn after these first sultry nights seems like the dreaming of the earth still continued into the daylight. I love that early twilight hour when the crickets still creak right on with such dewy faith and promise, as if it were still night, expressing the innocence of morning... The earth song of the cricket! Before Christianity was, it is."

One lives for walks.

"A walk through the woods was often my recreation. It was worth the while, if only to feel the wind blow on your cheek freely and see the waves run."

One lives for sparrows.

"I once had a sparrow alight upon my shoulder for a moment while I was hoeing in a village garden, and I felt that I was more distinguished by that circumstance than should have been by any epaulet I could have worn."

One lives for color.

"Already, by the first of September, I had seen two or three small maples turned scarlet across the pond, beneath where the white stems of three aspens diverged, at the point of a promontory, next to the water. Ah! Many a tale their color told. And gradually from week to week the character of each tree came out, and it admired itself reflected in the smooth mirror of the lake. Each morning the manager of this gallery substituted some new pictures, distinguished by more brilliant or harmonious coloring, for the old upon the walls."

Thoreau once said, "I would rather sit on a pumpkin and have it all to myself than to be crowded on a velvet cushion." "I have never found the companion that was so companionable as solitude." And again, " I have a great deal of company in my house; especially in the morning, when nobody calls."

Even Thoreau moved from his pond to be with friends in Concord. Over life's course, when problems arise, we need to have someone to lean upon and someone who can lean on us.

The ocean of sky overhead is not denied to anyone on earth. Many of its shows are spectacular. The arrival of dawn and dusk are always special. There can be cumulous clouds that match in beauty any snow-covered mountain range.

Take a good pair of binoculars into a clear night sky away from bright city lights. By looking up, one enters the universe — the constellations of stars in their hourly and seasonal changes. There are close to 3,000 stars visible to the naked eye at any one period of time. Constellation patterns never change. Most popular are the Great Bear — or Big Dipper, the Little Bear — or Little Dipper, The Swan, and the Square of Pegasus. With winter comes Orion the Hunter as a guide to other constellations. There are the planets that look like brilliant stars — Venus, Jupiter, the red tint of Mars, and the more elusive Saturn. Seen are the dark patches on the moon and on rare occasions meteors shooting across the sky. In the upper north latitudes at the equinoxes the Northern Lights are dazzling.

The following charts are drawn for the sky at about 9:00 PM in the middle of each season. Paths of the planets are indicated by shaded lines.

Constellations and Stars in the Northern Hemisphere

AUTUMN SKY

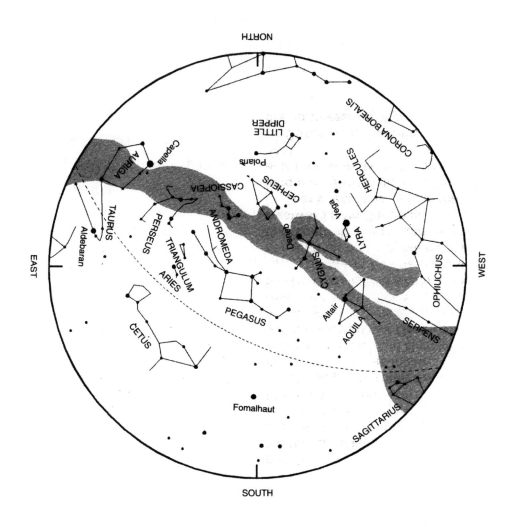

WINTER SKY

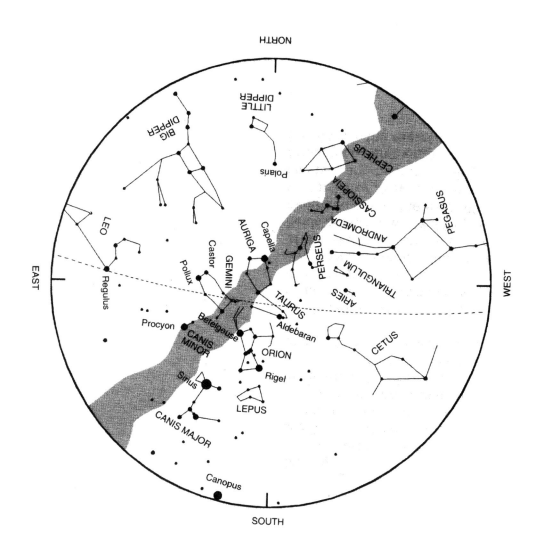

SPRING SKY

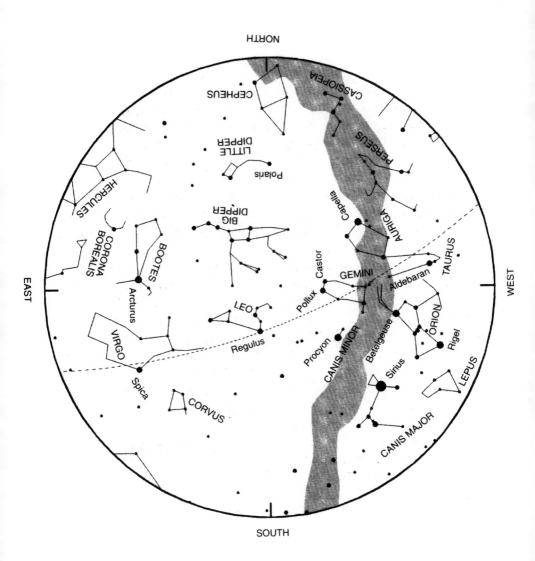

SUMMER SKY

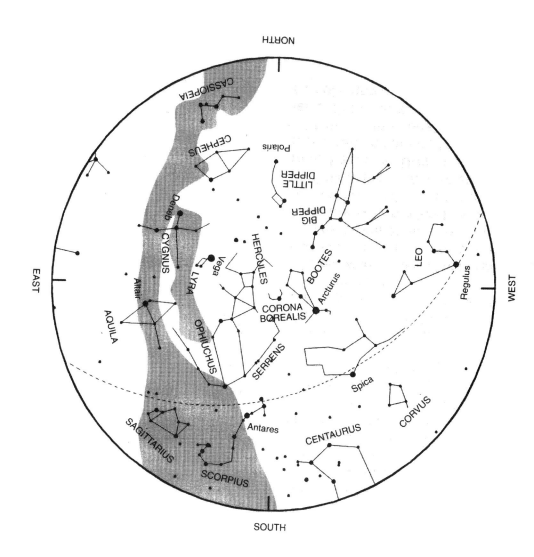

One can usually find a place of stillness for contemplation in each day and night. Silence, dancing leaves, waterfalls, mosses, hills, valleys, favorite smells — what unique pleasures for the asking. Every hour has a different mood. Ansel Adams, the celebrated photographer, said, "Contact with fundamental earthy things gives a startling perspective on the high-spun realities of modern life. Nature has no sense of sorrow about the past or anxiety about the future. When you look at nature you have to look around your mind. There's nothing between it and you. You look and begin to understand you are bigger than you were." Nature brings new friends and delight into our lives.

TRAVEL: PLEASURE VIA DONKEY OR
SEA FREIGHTER

With aging there is more time for travel. Travel offers adventure, novelty, education, culture, renewal, and fun. Traveling with a companion makes it doubly so.

For the greatest challenges there are the great national parks spreading from Acadia in Maine, a part of the Appalachian Trail in the Great Smoky Mountains to the Everglades in Florida; in the Midwest from Isle Royale in upper Michigan to the Badlands in South Dakota down to the San Antonio Missions; up the Continental Divide from the Saguaro in Arizona or donkey travel in the Grand Canyon to Yosemite in California or Glacier Park in Montana. Still in the confines of the United States there are nine national parks in Alaska, the largest being Wrangell-St. Elias covering over eight million acres. If homebound one can explore these parks in issues of the magazine National Geographic found in one's local library. Adopting one state per month, in four and one-half years one will have visited all 50 states.

To travel in the United States on wheels, find just the right time of year to visit favorite places—the Florida Keys in winter, Minnesota canoe country in summer, the Charleston, South Carolina azalea season or the Blue Ridge Parkway dogwoods in spring, or Vermont in early fall when the oaks and maples turn crimson and gold. One can manage all of these travels and more, including foreign country sights, sitting in one's easy chair, viewing selected rental videos.

Older travelers are venturing beyond traditional window bus tours. They are seeking new adventures in active exploration and learning. Some rent a car and take off exploring on their own. What is an Elderhostel? Elderhostel is a non-profit organization serving the needs of older adults. Many of Elderhostel's week long trips are held in hotels and motels, college dormitories, or conference centers. The group offers domestic trips and international expeditions, which are usually one to four weeks long. Service programs are also offered, with seniors volunteering with public service groups around the world. Current Elderhostel year-round catalogs are found in public libraries .

In the next ten years people over fifty will more than double, and they will be looking for new experiences. Elderhostel has 1,000 sites in the 50 states and Canada and in 37 countries abroad. What a way to discover new ideas and meet new friends! Elderhostels now offer the opportunity to include younger companions, for example, grandchildren ages 5 to 25. Elderhostel offers a few select programs that include amenities such as first class hotel accommodations, upscale dining, quality coach transport, and peak season locales.

Society Expeditions in Seattle offer courses worldwide with distinguished lecturers. The World Wildlife Fund has expeditions worldwide, as do Earthwatch and the National Geographic Society.

One can travel the world by freighter, seaport to seaport with a deck steward on call for any comfort. Small private cabins with amenities are available aboard freighters at reasonable cost. One eats with the captain at the captain's table. There are days ashore at ports of cargo delivery. At sea one relaxes topside in one's deck chair to read, to observe sea changes, sea birds, and weather changes. Observing the night sky can be spectacular with a 360-

degree view and no competing city lights. Examples of ports to visit are Caribbean islands, European ports, South America, Africa, Japan, China, Australia, New Zealand.

On some freighters there are a splash room and an exercise room. Some spend time writing with their laptops or doing handiwork. Board and card games are available. Often there are like-minded passengers for lively conversations. The top age may be 80. A sick bay is available with contact by radio with shore doctors. A full stock of pharmaceuticals is aboard. Another option is the University of Pittsburgh's SSP Universe, a floating campus with cruises as far as India. For further information a bi-monthly magazine Traveltips is available or by subscription.

Many elders make their own travel plans in a rented or owned light camper or a recreational vehicle. Even if the vehicle can tow only 3,000 pounds, there are trailers available complete with shower and a half tub, toilet, automatic furnace, a full kitchen, air conditioning, sitting and living space, plus beds sliding out at each end and the dinette converting to a bed as well. There is screening for warm weather, clear plastic sides that zip shut if it is cold or rainy, and a roll out awning for sunny days. Whatever the mode of travel, the world is there waiting to be explored.

THE PLEASURES OF READING

For fun reading one can always carry reading material in one's carrying bag to take advantage of the day's natural lulls. Tuck in an hour each day for a stretch of good reading or read 10 to 20 minutes before turning in each night. When one wakes up, he can head straight to a book until the day gets underway. On vacation one can head for the comfortable chairs in bookstores or in libraries for uninterrupted reading. Or how about airport layovers, or while awaiting lengthy car repairs, or jury duty, or using recorded books on trips when not driving? Some can even read while walking their pets. One can set a goal of 50 to 100 pages a day and be amazed at the added fun!

Sitting in one's favorite chair at home without going afield, one can find joy in reading aloud to relatives or friends. A small stack of good reads takes us to other worlds.

Just for fun one can read a book a month to share with others or exchange books read. Brian Lamb, an interviewer on Sunday night's C-Span's "Booknotes", discusses a challenging new book with its author for an hour each week. One can even be a history buff raconteur.

Here are some recommendations for information and fun:

The Quality of Life by James Michener

A High Old Time by Lavinia Russ

You and Your Will by Paul Ashley

Being a Widow by Lynn Caine

The View from 80 by Malcolm Cowley

30 Dirty Lies about Old by Hugh Downs

Our Best Years by Helen Hayes
It Takes a Long Time to Become Young by Garson Kanin

**A list of good books compiled by teacher-writer
Trudy Madden from Friendly, West Virginia
as presented to an Elderhostel at Camp Miniwanca
on the shores of Lake Michigan.**

Hard Times by Studs Terkel
Grandma Moses, My Life's Story by Anna Mary Moses
How to Write Your Own Life Story by Lois Daniel
Anything Can Happen by George Papashvily
Seven Winters and Afterthoughts by Elizabeth Bowen
Testament of Youth by Vera Brittain
All in a Lifetime by Frank Buck
I Have Known Many Worlds by Roger Burlingame
The Little Kingdom by Hughie Call
It's Good to Be Alive by Roy Campanella
My Autobiography by Charles Chaplin
I Remember It Well by Maurice Chevalier
On My Own by Eleanor Roosevelt
Myself Among Others by Ruth Gordon
A Joyful Noise by Janet Gillespie
Beyond Ourselves by Catherine Marshall
Story of My Life by Helen Keller
We by Charles Lindbergh
Our Hearts Were Young and Gay by Cornelia Otis Skinner
Drawn from Life by Ernest Shepherd
Portrait of Self by Margaret Bourke White

The Heart Is the Teacher by Covello Land

Only When I Laugh by Gladys Workman

To Me It's Wonderful by Ethel Waters

The Hiding Place by Corrie Ten Boom

Family Gathering by Kathleen Norris

Lonesome Traveler by Jack Kerouac

Travels with Charlie by John Steinbeck

Life Was Simpler Then by Louis Erdman

On Reflection by Helen Hayes

One Writer's Beginnings by Eudora Welty

An Autobiography by Agatha Christie

Autobiography by Benjamin Franklin

Drink the Dipper Dry by Jerrod Metz

A Bridge Through Time by Laila Said

Galina; a Russian Story by Galina Vishnevskaya

The Road from Coorain and *True North* by Jill Ker Conway

Me by Katherine Hepburn

Bearing Witness edited by Henry Louis Gates

The Bookmaker's Daughter by Shirley Abbott

Write the Story of Your life by Ruth Kanin

Preserving your Past by Janice Dixon & Dora Flack

First Confessions by Frank O'Connor

A list of fun authors prepared by Elizabeth Douvan, retired Professor of Psychology and Women's Studies at the University of Michigan. She said, "these are books to be read now with more time in retirement."

MYSTERIES
Janwillem Van de Wetering
Maj Sjowall
Per Wahloo
Dick Francis
Tony Hellerman
Sara Peretsky
Sue Grafton
Robert Campbell

GENERAL
Jane Austin
Virginia Woolf
Emily Dickinson
David McClelland
Victor Turner
Herbert Gans
Joyce Ladner
Lillian Rubin
Nancy Chodoroff

INSIGHTS
Childhood and Society
   by Erik Erickson
Go Tell it to the Mountain
   by JamesBaldwin

GHOST WRITERS
Philip Roth
Isabel Allende
Wole Soyinka
Wallace Stegner
Iris Murdoch

SCIENCE FICTION
Issac Asimov
Ray Bradbury
Authur Clarke
Michael Crichton
Robert A. Heinlein

CHILDREN'S STORIES
E. Nesbitt
E.B. White

WOMEN WRITERS

Maya Angelou

Phyllis Rose

Nina Auerbach

Mary O'Brien

Catherine Mac Kinnon

Natalie Davis

Bell Hooks

Sara Maitland

Lara Evans

Toni Morrison

Maxine Hong Kingston

Alice Walker

Margaret Drable

Margaret Lawrence

Alice Munro

Alice Adams

Mary Gordon

AUTOBIOGRAPHY

From Time to Time by Hanna Tillich

Ursula LeGuin (essays)

NOVELS

The Magic Mountain by Thomas Mann

Brothers Karamazov by Fyodor Dostoyevsky

Jude the Obscure by Thomas Hardy

Modern Library has listed the great novels in English of the 20th century:

Ulysses by James Joyce
The Great Gatsby by F. Scott Fitzgerald
A Portrait of the Artist as a Young Man by James Joyce
Lolita by Vladimir Nabokov
Brave New World by Aldous Huxley
The Sound and the Fury by James Faulkner
Catch-22 by Joseph Heller
Darkness at Noon by Arthur Koestler
Sons and Lovers by D.H. Lawrence
The Grapes of Wrath by John Steinbeck
Under the Volcano by Malcolm Lowry
The Way of All Flesh by Samuel Butler
1984 by George Orwell
I, Claudius by Robert Graves
To the Lighthouse by Virginia Woolf
An American Tragedy by Theodore Dreiser
The Heart is a Lonely Hunter by Carson McCullers
Slaughterhouse Five by Kurt Vonnegut,Jr.
Invisible Man by Ralph Ellison
Native Son by Richard Wright
Henderson the Rain King by Saul Bellow
Appointment in Samarra by John O'Hara
*U S.A. (*Trilogy*)* by John Dos Passos
Winesburg,Ohio by Sherwood Anderson
A Passage to India by E.M. Forster
The Wings of the Dove by Henry James

The Ambassadors by Henry James

Tender Is the Night by F. Scott Fitzgerald

Studs Lonigan (Trilogy) by James T. Farrell

The Good Soldier by Ford Madox Ford

Animal Farm by George Orwell

The Golden Bowl by Henry James

Sister Carrie by Theodore Dreiser

A Handful of Dust by Evelyn Waugh

As I Lay Dying by William Faulkner

All the King's Men by Robert Penn Warren

The Bridge of San Luis Rey by Thorton Wilder

Howard's End by E.M. Forster

Go Tell it on the Mountain by James Baldwin

The Heart of the Matter by Graham Greene

Lord of the Flies by William Golding

Deliverance by James Dickey

A Dance to the Music of Time by Anthony Powell

Point Counter Point by Aldous Huxley

The Sun Also Rises by Ernest Hemingway

The Secret Agent by Joseph Conrad

Nostromo by Joseph Conrad

The Rainbow by D.H. Lawrence

Women in Love by D.H. Lawrence

Tropic of Cancer by Henry Miller

The Naked and the Dead by Norman Mailer

Portnoy's Complaint by Philip Roth

Pale Fire by Vladimir Nabokov

Light in August by William Faulkner

On the Road by Jack Kerouac

The Maltese Falcon by Dashiell Hammett
Parade's End by Ford Madox Ford
The Age of Innocence by Edith Wharton
Zuleika Dobson by Max Beerbohm
The Moviegoer by Walker Percy
Death Comes for the Archbishop by Willa Cather
From Here to Eternity by James Jones
The Wapshot Chronicle by John Cheever
The Catcher in the Rye by J.D. Salinger
A Clockwork Orange by Anthony Burgess
Of Human Bondage by Somerset Maugham
Heart of Darkness by Joseph Conrad
Main Street by Sinclair Lewis
The House of Mirth by Edith Wharton
The Alexandria Quartet by Lawrence Durrell
A High Wind in Jamaica by Richard Hughes
A House for Mr. Biswas by V. S. Naipaul
The Day of the Locust by Nathaniel West
A Farewell to Arms by Ernest Hemingway
Scoop by Evelyn Waugh
The Prime of Miss Jean Brodie by Muriel Spark
Finnegans Wake by James Joyce
Kim by Rudyard Kipling
A Room with a View by E. M. Forster
Brideshead Revisited by Evelyn Waugh

Modern Library has listed the best non-fiction:

The Education of Henry Adams by Henry Adams
The Varieties of Religious Experience by William James
Up from Slavery by Booker T. Washington
A Room of One's Own by Virginia Woolf
Silent Spring by Rachel Carson
Selected Essays, 1917-1932 by T.S. Eliot
The Double Helix by James D. Watson
Speak, Memory by Vladimir Nabokov
The American Language by H.L. Mencken
The General Theory of Employment, Interest, and Money
    by John Maynard Keynes
The Lives of a Cell by Lewis Thomas
The Frontier in American History by Frederick Jackson Turner
Black Boy by Richard Wright
Aspects of the Novel by E.M. Forster
The Civil War by Shelby Foote
The Guns of August by Barbara W. Tuchman
The Proper Study of Mankind by Isaiah Berlin
The Nature and Destiny of Man by Reinhold Neibuhr
Notes of a Native Son by James Baldwin
The Autobiography of Alice B. Toklas by Gertrude Stein
The Elements of Style by William Strunk and E.B. White
An American Dilemma by Gunnar Myrdal
Principia Mathematica by Alfred North Whitehead
    and Bertrand Russell
The Mismeasure of Man by Stephen Jay Gould
The Mirror and the Lamp by Meyer Howard Abrams

The Art of the Soluble by Peter B. Medawar

The Ants by Bert Hoelldobler and Edward O. Wilson

A Theory of Justice by John Rawls

Art and Illusion by Ernest H. Gombrich

The Making of the English Working Class by E.P.Thompson

The Souls of Black Folk by W.E.B. DuBois

Principia Ethica by G.E. Moore

Philosophy and Civilization by John Dewey

On Growth and Form by D'Arcy Wentworth Thompson

Ideas and Opinions by Albert Einstein

The Age of Jackson by Arthur M. Schlesinger, Jr.

The Making of the Atomic Bomb by Richard Rhodes

Black Lamb and Grey Falcon by Rebecca West

Autobiographies by W. B. Yeats

Science and Civilization in China by Joseph Needham

Goodbye to All That by Robert Graves

Homage to Catalonia by George Orwell

The Autobiography of Mark Twain by Mark Twain

Children of Crisis by Robert Coles

A Study of History by Arnold J. Toynbee

The Affluent Society by John Kenneth Galbraith

Present at the Creation by Dean Acheson

The Great Bridge by David McCullough

Patriotic Gore by Edmund Wilson

Samuel Johnson by Walter Jackson Bate

The Autobiography of Malcolm X by Alex Haley and Malcolm X

The Right Stuff by Tom Wolfe

Eminent Victorians by Lytton Strachey

Working by Studs Terkel

Darkness Visible by William Styron

The Liberal Imagination by Lionel Trilling

The Second World War by Winston Churchill

Out of Africa by Isak Dinesen

Jefferson and His Times by Dumas Malone

In the American Grain by William Carlos Williams

Cadillac Desert by Marc Reisner

The House of Morgan by Ron Chernow

The Sweet Science by A.J. Leibling

The Open Society and Its Enemies by Karl Popper

The Art of Memory by Frances A. Yates

Religion and the Rise of Capitalism by R.H. Tawney

A Preface to Morals by Walter Lippmann

The Gate of Heavenly Peace by Jonathan D. Spence

The Structure of Scientific Revolutions by Thomas S. Kuhn

The Strange Career of Jim Crow by C. Vann Woodward

The Rise of the West by William H. McNeill

The Gnostic Gospels by Elaine Pagels

James Joyce by Richard Ellmann

Florence Nightingale by Cecil Woodham-Smith

The Great War and Modern Memory by Paul Fussell

The City in History by Lewis Mumford

Battle Cry of Freedom by James M. McPherson

Why We Can't Wait by Martin Luther King Jr.

The Rise of Theodore Roosevelt by Edmund Morris

Studies in Iconology by Erwin Panofsky

The Face of Battle by John Keegan

The Strange Death of Liberal England by George Dangerfield

Vermeer by Lawrence Gowing

A Bright Shining Lie by Neil Sheehan

West with the Night by Beryl Markham

This Boy's Life by Tobias Wolff

A Mathematician's Apology by G.H. Hardy

Six Easy Pieces by Richard P. Feynman

Pilgrim at Tinker Creek by Annie Dillard

The Golden Bough by James George Frazer

Shadow and Act by Ralph Ellison

The Power Broker by Robert A. Caro

The American Political Tradition by Richard Hofstadter

The Contours of American History by William Appleman Williams

The Promise of American Life by Herbert Croly

In Cold Blood by Truman Capote

The Journalist and the Murderer by Janet Malcolm

The Taming of Chance by Ian Hacking

Operating Instructions by Anne Lamott

Melbourne by Lord David Cecil

LARGE PRINT TITLES

GENERAL FICTION

Assignment in Brittany by Helen MacInnes

Beloved by Toni Morrison

Cimarron by Edna Ferber

East of Eden by John Steinbeck

The Hundred Secrets by Amy Tan

The Kentuckians by Janis Holt Giles

Ladder of Years by Anne Tyler

Lady of Quality by Georgette Heyer

Lake Wobegon Days by Garrison Keillor

Love is Eternal by Irving Stone

The Mother by Pearl Buck

Recessional by James Michener

MYSTERIES AND SUSPENSE

Airframe by Michael Crichton

The Best Man to Die by Ruth Rendell

Blood Shot by Sara Paretsky

The Cat Who Went Underground by Lillian Jackson Braun

Chamelon by William Kienzle

Dead Man's Folly by Agatha Christie

Flying Finish by Dick Francis

Hangman's Holiday by Dorothy Sayers

Inspector Queen's Own Case by Ellery Queen

Knock on Death's Door by Ellis Peters

A Mind to Murder by P.D. James

Mrs. Pollifax and the Golden Triangle by Dorothy Gilman

NATURE, SCIENCE AND GEOGRAPHY
Blue Highways by William Heat Moon
A Brief History of Time by S.W. Hawking
Drums Along the Amazon by Victor G. Norwood
From the Ocean to the Sky by Edmund Hillary
The Immortal Wilderness by John Hay
In Praise of Seasons by Alan Olmstead
The Kingdom by the Sea by Paul Theroux
The Lost World of the Kalahari by Laurens Van der Post
Return to Tibet by Heinrich Harrer
The Whispering Land by Gerald Durrell

BIOGRAPHY
Adventures in Two Worlds by A.J. Cronin
Being Seventy by Elizabeth Gray Vining
Gandhi, His Life and Message by Louis Fischer
Growing Up by Russell Baker
Jack Benny by Irving A. Fein
My American Journey by Colin Powell
Notable Men and Women of the Civil War by Jean Robbitscher
A Reporter's Life by Walter Cronkite
Tracy and Hepburn by Garson Kanin
Women of Courage by Margaret Truman

HOBBIES
Healthy Houseplants A to Z by Anita Guyton
An Older Woman's Health Guide by Joan Mintz
Pets and Their People by Bruce Fogle
Vegetable Growing by Fred Loads
Window Box Gardening by Roy Genders

RELIGION AND INSPIRATION

Beyond Ourselves by Catherine Marshall

A Celebration of Life by Norman Cousins

Everything to Gain by Jimmy Carter

The Virtues of Aging by Jimmy Carter

Gift from the Sea by Anne Morrow Lindbergh

No Man Is an Island by Thomas Merton

Peace with God by Billy Graham

Pulling Your Own Strings by Wayne W. Dyer

A Simple Path by Mother Teresa

Yes, You Can by Art G. Linkletter

You Can If You Think You Can by Norman Vincent Peale

MISCELLANEOUS

The Random House *Large Print Book of Jokes & Anecdotes*

The Random House *Large Print Treasury of Best Loved Poems*

Women are using life writing as a means of self-understanding and a connection with the past, present, and the future. Some examples:

Diary of a Young Girl by Anne Frank

Women's Life Writing by Linda Coleman

Women's Way of Knowing by Mary Belenky

Tapestries of Life by Bettina Aptheker

The Private Self by Shari Benstock

Essays on Life Writing by Marlene Kadar

The Female Autograph by Donna Stanton

The Life of an Ordinary Woman by Anne Ellis

Daniel Boorstin, former Librarian of Congress, recommends books that every American should read. There follow three from his list:

1. *Undaunted Courage: Meriwether Lewis, Thomas Jefferson and the Opening of the American West*
   by Stephen Ambrose
2. *Stars in Their Course: The Gettysburg Campaign*
   by Shelby Foote
3. *No Ordinary Time* by Doris K. Goodwin

One can increase reading speed by scanning for key words. Reading for 25 minutes a day at 300 words per minute means one reads 52,500 words a week, 210,000 a month, 2,520,000 words a year, about 800 books per year. That's almost eight times the average read by public library borrowers in the United States. It becomes easy to become well-read. Reading a significant number of the books listed might equal a college major in literature. Fun, relaxation, and restoration are found in moments of reading.

STORIES AND JOKES

One can collect a repertoire of jokes and stories. With apology for any that may be offensive, the author retells a few.

Politics:

The difference between Democrats and Republicans is that Democrats eat the fish they catch; Republicans mount them on the wall!

Republicans date women who are Democrats but marry Republicans. They feel they are entitled to a little fun first!

Aging:

She reminisced to her husband, "You used to kiss me."
So he leaned over and kissed her. "You used to hold my hand." So he reached over and held her hand. "You used to bite me warmly on the back of the neck." Pause. "Where are you going?"

He, "To get my teeth. I left them in the bathroom."

Cancelled Flight:

The airline flight agent faced a long line of disgruntled passengers trying to rebook tickets. A man burst into the front of the line and demanded, "I have to be on this flight, and I have to be in first class."

The attendant politely asked him to get in line and that she would help him when his turn came.

He shouted back, "Do you know who I am?"

She smiled, picked up the microphone and announced, "We have a passenger who does not know who he is. If anyone can help him, please come to the gate."

The passenger, now enraged by the laughter of people around him, glared at the agent and swore, "Screw you!"

Without missing a beat, the agent smiled, picked up her microphone, "I'm sorry, sir, you will have to get in line for that too."

The people in line burst into cheers as the passenger bolted, cursing the agent.

Ministers out of the pulpit and sometimes in the pulpit can be the source of humorous stories.

The Church on Fire

The Presbyterians appointed a chairperson to appoint a committee to make a report to the session.

The Methodists gathered in the corner to pray.

The Catholics passed the collection basket to cover damages.

The Baptists cried, "Where is the water?"

The Lutherans posted a notice on the door declaring that fire was evil.

The Fundamentalists proclaimed, "It's Heaven's vengeance."

The Quakers quietly praised the heavens for the blessing fire brings.

The Congregationalists shouted, "Every man for himself."

The Episcopalians formed a procession and marched out.

The Unitarians had a party.

The disbelievers jumped into the fire to see if it was real!

The New Minister's Arrival

The new minister in town was immediately put on the spot

when the young married couples' class requested a Friday night talk on how to handle sex. The minister asked his wife if she was coming. She replied that she was too busy getting settled, but what was he going to talk about? Embarrassed to tell her, he parried the question, saying he thought he might talk about sailing.

The morning after the talk the minister's wife while out shopping met a young woman of the congregation who was effusive about the minister's talk. The minister's wife replied, "He really doesn't know much about it. The first time he got seasick and the second time his hat blew off."

The ability to tell a good story or folk tale can be nurtured. When people laugh together, there is a feeling of connection, a sense of belonging to one another.

DANCING FOR WALLFLOWERS:
SQUARE. SINGLE, OR LINE

Square dancing requires lots of people, a large room, and a caller. Single and line dancing are fun and can be participated in almost anywhere by all ages that can walk without assistance. There is magic in dance, supplying a need for self-expression while enjoying activity with others. It does require counting in sequence, coordinating body movement and the mind together. Where else can one express oneself in unison with others in such an easy and orderly way?

"The Grapevine" is a simple solo dance to the tune of the song, *The Jolly Woodpecker*.

> Step right – toe tap – heel tap
> Step left – toe tap – heel tap
> Three steps back, swing 45 degrees and repeat
> the above
> Do three times more to complete the four directions.
> Repeat as desired.

"The Honky Tonk Twist" is another solo or line dance.

HONKY TONK TWIST

Swivel Heels: 1 - 4

Feet together, transfer weight slightly to balls of feet and swivel heels:

1. To the left
2. Hold
3. To the right
4. Hold

Twist: 5 - 8

Feet together, transfer weight slightly to balls of feet and twist heels:

5. To the left
6. To the right
7. To the left
8. To the right

Heel/Toe Taps: 1 - 4

1. & 2. Tap right heel forward twice
3. & 4. Tap right toe backward twice

Slide-Locks: 1 - 6

1. & 2. Step forward with right, slide lock left behind it
3. & 4. Step forward with right, slide lock left behind it
5. & 6. Right step forward and kick out with left doing half-turn to the right

Slide/Locks: 1 - 6

1. & 2. Step forward with left, slide lock right behind it
3. & 4. Step forward with left, slide lock right behind it
5. & 6. Left step forward and kick out with right doing half-turn to the left

Vine With a Half-turn: 1- 4

1. Right step to the right
2. Left step behind right
3. Do foot position to the right with right foot
4. Do half-turn to the right with a brush

Vine To The Left: 5 - 8

5. Left step to the left
6. Right step behind left
7. Left step to the left
8. Bring right next to left with a stomp

In the Macarena Dance one can stand in one place and do it alone or with others.

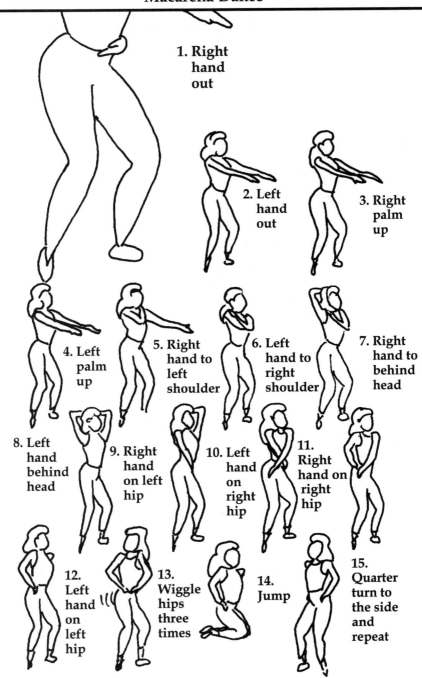

1. Right hand out

2. Left hand out

3. Right palm up

4. Left palm up

5. Right hand to left shoulder

6. Left hand to right shoulder

7. Right hand to behind head

8. Left hand behind head

9. Right hand on left hip

10. Left hand on right hip

11. Right hand on right hip

12. Left hand on left hip

13. Wiggle hips three times

14. Jump

15. Quarter turn to the side and repeat

The "Zorba Dance" uses Greek music and is for any number of people.

> Start with feet together
> One toe goes out, one toe goes in
> Then fingers begin to snap
> And we add a step and a tap
> Take a step, then a kick
> Two steps back, but not too quick
> Now we're dancing in a line
> Arms on shoulders all entwined
> Right foot crosses, one and two
> Then the left one you must do
> Then once again our fingers snap
> And we do the step and tap
> Then our toes go out and in
> And once again our dance begins (but faster)
> Our hands go up
> Our knees will bend
> And slowly that's how Zorba dance will end.

Line dancing can use the music of Glenn Miller, The Barnum and Bailey Band, or other favorites. Place hands on the waist of the forward person and take three steps forward and kick right, then three steps forward and kick left. A leader using arm movements can remind the dancers which direction to kick.

International and intergenerational dancing is bonding and one of the most beautiful fun things initiated by the aging. It sustains the fullness and wholesomeness of life.

SINGING AND LISTENING TO OLD AND NEW SONGS

A great fun function is found in song, unleashing freedom 60 to 100+. Our favorites have many origins during many centuries. In the mid 1700s an English slave trader, John Newton, scribed *Amazing Grace* in a terrible storm on the way to America as all on board prepared to die in the storm.

Amazing Grace

Amazing grace, how sweet the sound
That saved a wretch like me.
I once was lost but now am found,
Was blind but now I see.

Through many dangers, toils and snares
I have already come;
'Tis grace has brought me safe thus far
And grace will lead me home.

The Lord has promised good to me,
His word my hope secures;
He will my shield and portion be
As long as life endures, long as life endures.

The travelers survived, and John Newton later became a minister.

Folk singers in America crisscrossed the country expressing

joy through their songs. Among them are Pete Seeger, Joan Baez, and Woody Guthrie. There follows one of their best-known songs, *This Land Is Your Land:*

Chorus: *This land is your land, this land is my land*
From California to the New York Island
From the redwood forests, to the Gulf Stream waters
This land was made for you and me.

1. *As I was walking that ribbon of highway, I saw above me the endless skyway*
I saw below me that golden valley, this land was made for you and me.

2. *I've roamed and rambled, I've followed my footsteps, to the sparkling sands of her diamond deserts;*
And all around me a voice was sounding: this land Was made for you and me.

Chorus:

3. *When the sun came shining, and I was strolling, and the wheat fields waving, and the dust clouds rolling As the fog was lifting, a voice was chanting: this land was made for you and me.*

4. *Nobody living can ever stop me, as I go walking that freedom highway;*
Nobody living can make me turn back: this land was made for you and me.

Chorus

One can relax with recordings of Glenn Miller, Les Brown, Jimmy Dorsey, Sammy Kay, Duke Ellington, Artie Shaw, Count Basie, Kay Kayser, Hal Kemp, And Harry James.

One never forgets *The White Cliffs of Dover, When the Lights Go on Again All Over the World, Don't Fence Me In, Sally, Sally of My Dreams, I'll Be Seeing You, Dancing in the Dark, That Old Black Magic,* or *By the Light of the Silvery Moon.*

Many American folk songs originated in black churches during slavery. There is a lode of great music in Negro spirituals, blues, ballads, and jazz. The song *Lift Up Ev'ry Voice and Sing* is a classic for all to voice their deepest emotions and aspirations in the name of freedom.

FILMS

For Fun Function there follow some 100 selected all-time best movies available at neighborhood video stores.

Abe Lincoln in Illinois
African Queen
Alexander's Ragtime Band
All about Eve
All Quiet on the Western Front
American in Paris
Annie Hall
The Apartment
Apocalypse Now

Ben Hur
The Best Years of our Lives
Bonnie and Clyde
Birth of a Nation
Bridge Over the River Kwai
Bringing Up Baby
Butch Cassidy and the Sundance Kid

Cabaret
Casablanca
Chariots of Fire
Chinatown
Citizen Kane
City Lights

Crimes of the Heart
Crocodile Dundee

Dance of the White Dog
Dances with Wolves
The Desert Fox
Dog Man
Doctor Zhivago
Don Quixote
Double Indemnity
Dr. Jekyll and Mr. Hyde
Dr. Strangelove
Duck Soup

Educating Rita

From Here to Eternity

Gigi
The Golden Age of Comedy
Gone with the Wind
The Graduate
Grumpy Old Men

Hard Day's Night
High Noon
Hobson's Choice
Horse Feathers
Horse Whisperers

I Love You Again
The Inspector General
It Happened One Night
It's a Wonderful Life

Jane Eyre
Julia Misbehaves

The Last Picture Show
Laurel and Hardy Classics
The Lavender Hill Mob
Lawrence of Arabia
Libelled Lady
Lion in Winter
The Little Foxes
Little Women
The Long Hot Summer
The Longest Day
Love in the Afternoon

Maltese Falcon
The Man in the White Suit
The Man Who Came to Dinner
The Manchurian Candidate
M*A*S*H* Goodbye
The Matchmaker
The Mating Game
Midnight
Midnight Cowboy

My Fair Lady
My Favorite Wife
My Little Chickadee
My Man Godfrey

Network
New York Stories
No Time for Sergeants
North by Northwest

On Golden Pond
On the Waterfront
Otello

The Paleface
Phantom of the Opera
The Philadelphia Story
Play It Again, Sam
Plaza Suite
Psycho
The Purple Rose of Cairo
Pygmalion

The Quiet Man

Revenge of the Pink Panther
Roxie Hart
Ruggles of Red Gap

Sabrina

Schlindler's List

Searchers

The Secret Life of Walter Mitty

The Seven Year Itch

She Done Him Wrong

Show Boat

Silver Streak

Singin' in the Rain

Some Like It Hot

Son of the Morning Star

Sons of the Desert

The Sound of Music

Sounder

Splash

Stagecoach

Stage Door

Star Wars

Sunset Boulevard

The Sunshine Boys

Sweeney Todd

Sweet Charity

The Thin Blue Line

The Third Man

A Thousand Clowns

To Kill a Mockingbird

Tom Jones

Tootsie

Trouble with Harry
Two for the Road
2001: a Space Odyssey
Turtle Diary

West Side Story
When Comedy Was King
Will Success Spoil Rock Hunter
The Wizard of Oz
Wuthering Heights

Yankee Doodle Dandy

FUN AND GAMES WHEREVER YOU ARE, INDOORS OR OUT

Games can be played from ages 4 to 120, even with a walker or a wheelchair indoors, in a yard, or any nearby green space or park. They have been played worldwide for hundreds of years. There is croquet from France, bocci from Italy (lawn bowling), and tennis from Britain (can be practiced singly against a wall). More examples are darts from England, haggis sack from Scotland, hard and soft baseball from the United States, volleybird from Brazil, and tumbling from the Middle East.

Horseshoes are universal. Shuffleboard can be marked off on indoor halls or outdoor sidewalks. All ages can participate together in tug of war with equally divided sides by age and weight.

Kites can bring one close to nature, are safe, silent, nonpolluting, and sometimes spiritual in nature. When kites take to the air, heads turn upward. They appeal to the broadest spectrum of ages from 6 to 60 to 120 and are cheaper than a psychiatrist in one's search for sanity. One may never pilot a plane but can be at the controls of a tethered aircraft. Possibly the first use of a kite was by a Chinese general, Han Hain, in 200 BC to calculate the distance of an enemy's fortress walls, so he could dig a tunnel underneath them.

The history of kites continues to fascinate. Chinese General Huan Hsing, surrounded by enemies, attached noisemakers to kites and sent them flying over enemy lines, startling the enemy into mad retreat. Samoans used huge kites to pull their canoes. Koreans used kites for trolling to catch fish. Some of the earliest Chinese and Japanese kites were known to be 65 feet high, weighing nearly a ton. The bamboo supports of kites were perforated to make the wind whistle through them. These musical wind harps were flown from rooftops at night to ward off evil spirits.

Kite contests were held in Southeast Asia. A popular sport was to glue broken glass to the kite strings so that when one kite overtook another, it would cut it down.

In 1752 Benjamin Franklin flew his kites in thunderstorms and discovered electricity. Box kites paved the way for the Wright brothers to develop airplane flight. In World War II allied airmen who had been shot down over the sea used kites for sending distress signals. German U-boats lifted up observers in kites flown from their conning towers. A group of children here in the United States launched a train of 19 small kites on ten miles of line. In seven hours their kites reached 35,531 feet.

There are kite-flying skills. A proper tail keeps a kite upright and well balanced. The tail can be too short. Preferably it is six times the length of the kite. To make the tail shorter, attach bows every four to eight inches. Without a proper tail, the kite will spin all over the sky and crash into the ground.

Skills in kite flying need not require running with the kite. Walk backward with the kite to make it rise; walk toward it to make it dive or somersault. One can judge the wind as follows:

1-3 miles – smoke drifts

4 –6 miles – leaves on trees rustle, wind is felt on face
(preferable)

7-10 miles – leaves in motion

11-15 miles – small branches move, dust is raised

To launch a kite have someone walk or run under it sliding a gloved hand along the string. To reel the kite in, walk toward the kite. To create aerobatics in flight, let out more line rapidly or take several steps toward the kite. Never fly a kite in wet weather. The wet line is a conductor of electricity built up in clouds. Once airborne a kite can be tied to a beach chair and it will fly itself for hours. If a kite dips deeply, let out some string and then quickly reel in the slack.

Given an open space and a 5 mile mph wind, dancing with the clouds is a kind of choreography! One has control; the partner is in the sky. The object is to keep it fun. Stay away from trees and power lines at a distance as least as great as the length of the kite's string. It makes more sense to spend $15.00 on a kite that will last. Once the kite is bought, unless you make your own, the fuel is free!

The boomerang from Australian ancestry is a fun game wherever there is grass and no trees. The boomerang was first used by the aborigines for hunting small game and birds. Now they are made of plastic, from plywood, or in a high tech composite. The aerobatic principle is a whirling airfoil lifted through rotation. An experienced thrower with calm, cool, dry air can loft a boomerang 100 feet high. The official time record in the air, set in Ohio, is 17 minutes. The boomerang hovered over a river, caught an updraft, then went over a highway traveling probably for a mile blowing back to the thrower who caught it.

Throwing a boomerang:

If the boomerang does not make a complete return, but circles in front of you, try tilting it a few more degrees to the right. You may have to tilt it as much as 45 or 50 degrees.

If the boomerang lands behind you on a calm day, try throwing with less force. If this doesn't work, try holding it more vertically and releasing it at a higher angle.

The best time to throw a boomerang is on a calm day, when there is no more than a breeze from 3 to 5 miles an hour.

The illustration on the previous page shows how to hold a boomerang. The flat side is against the palm of the hand with the rounded side facing you. The elbow of the boomerang should point over your shoulder. This is the classic Australian Aboriginal hold. When correctly held, the tip of the boomerang should be about 2 inches below the thumb. The thumb should lay across the boomerang at right angles to it and the index finger should overlap the boomerang. It is the index finger which trips the boomerang to give it spin when thrown.

You should always face the wind when throwing and never throw downwind. Standing facing the wind, turn about 45 degrees to your right so the wind is on your left cheek. This way you allow the boomerang to circle around and return to you from the left side.

THE ACTOR IN YOU: ROLE PLAYING OR GROUP PANTOMIME WITH A READER

Many well-known plays have great parts for the elderly. An example is the role of Grandpa in the classic play, *You Can't Take It with You.*

Women can create skits in which they don elaborate hats and create nonsense — having a tea party or visiting an ice cream parlor.

A good act for men is pantomiming Robert Service's poem *The Shooting of Dan McGrew* at a mock Klondike saloon with a reader in the background telling the story and furnishing sound effects.

The Shooting of Dan McGrew

A bunch of the boys were whooping it up in the Malamute
    saloon;
The kid that handles the music-box was hitting a jag-time tune;
Back of the bar, in a solo game, sat Dangerous Dan McGrew,
And watching his luck was his light-o'-love, the lady that's
    known as Lou.

When out of the night, which was fifty below, and into the din
    and the glare,
There stumbled a miner fresh from the creeks, dog-dirty, and
    loaded for bear.
He looked like a man with a foot in the grave and scarcely the
    strength of a louse,
Yet he tilted a poke of dust on the bar, and he called for drinks
    for the house.

There was none could place the stranger's face, though we
  searched ourselves for a clue;
But we drank his health, and the last to drink was Dangerous
  Dan McGrew.

There's men that somehow just grip your eyes, and hold them
  hard like a spell;
And such was he, and he looked to me like a man who had
  lived in hell;
With a face most hair, and the dreary stare of a dog whose day
  is done,
As he watered the green stuff in his glass, and the drops fell
  one by one.
Then I got to figgering who he was, and wondering what he'd
  do,
And I turned my head — and there watching him was the lady
  that's known as Lou.

His eyes went rubbering round the room, and he seemed in a
  kind of daze,
Till at last that old piano fell in the way of his wandering gaze.
The rag-time kid was having a drink; there was no one else on
  the stool,
So the stranger stumbles across the room, and flops down there
  like a fool.
In a buckskin shirt that was glazed with dirt he sat, and I saw
  him sway;
Then he clutched the keys with his talon hands — my God! But
  that man could play.

148

Were you ever out in the Great Alone, when the moon was
    awful clear,
    And the icy mountains hemmed you in with a silence you most
        could hear;
    With only the howl of a timber wolf, and you camped there in
        the cold,
    A half-dead thing in a stark, dead world, clean mad for the
        muck called gold;
    While high overhead, green, yellow, and red, the North Lights
        swept in bars? —
    Then you've a hunch what the music meant.... hunger and night
        and the stars.

    And hunger not of the belly kind, that's banished with bacon
        and beans,
    But the gnawing hunger of lonely men for a home and all that
        it means;
    For a fireside far from the cares that are, four walls and a roof
        above;
    But oh! so cramful of cozy joy, and crowned with a woman's
        love —
    A woman dearer than all the world, and true as Heaven is true
    (God! how ghastly she looks through her rouge, — the lady
        that's known as Lou....)

    The music almost died away.... then it burst like a pent-up flood;
    And it seemed to say, "Repay, repay," and my eyes were blind
        with blood.

The thought came back of an ancient wrong, and it stung like
   a frozen lash,
And the lust awoke to kill, to kill .....then the music stopped
   with a crash,
And the stranger turned, and his eyes they burned in a most
   peculiar way;
In a buckskin shirt that was glazed with dirt he sat, and I saw
   him sway;
Then his lips went in in a kind of grin, and he spoke, and his
   voice was calm,
And "Boys," says he, "you don't know me, and none of you
   care a damn;
But I want to state, and my words are straight, and I'll bet my
   poke they're true,
That one of you is a hound of hell.... and that one is Dan
   McGrew."

Then I ducked my head, and the lights went out, and two guns
   blazed in the dark,
And a woman screamed, and the lights went up, and two men
   lay stiff and stark.
Pitched on his head, and pumped full of lead, was Dangerous
   Dan McGrew,
While the man from the creeks lay clutched to the breast of the
   lady that's known as Lou.....
The woman that kissed him and – pinched his poke – was the
   lady that's known as Lou.

REDEFINING SEX FOR FUN

A person is not unhealthy or in need of medical treatment if he/she does not feel the need to have sex regularly. Sex is a short pleasure. Many find hobbies more lasting.

A degree of impotency is expected in aging. According to a 1999 report in <u>The Journal of the American Medical Association,</u> in later age more than 43% of women and 31% of men regularly have no interest in sex, cannot have an orgasm, or suffer from some other sexual dysfunction. Problems can arise with side effects from taking certain drugs.

For some with dysfunction, new drugs, such as *Viagra* at $10.00 a shot or *Muse* at $20.00 can help. These must be prescribed by one's doctor to solve specific problems and to avoid possible side effects.

Traditional sex may become optional in aging with substitute activities to express a loving relationship. Holding hands, hugs, snuggling, caressing, foot rubs, back rubs, kissing of the hands, arms, face, neck, shoulders, and back are all sexy.

In a Sex Survey by the National Institute of Mental Health loving family and financial security rated much higher than a satisfying sex life. Age was not found to be a factor in the importance attached to sexual satisfaction. Sex problems were frequent for only a minuscule number in the Survey.

Renewal comes from mutual caring and the sharing of one's closest feelings with others. These can be quiet dinners, mood music, good talk, and the celebration of birthdays and holidays. Planning good times together keeps the spark alive, whether with a live mate or with very close friends. Isolation is not healthy.

Even Thoreau moved from his pond to be with friends in Concord. Over life's course, when problems arise, we need to have someone to lean upon and someone who can lean on us.

OUR BEST FRIENDS: PETS —
REAL OR NON-REAL AT ONE'S FEET

Get a pet. Studies show that people who own pets have significantly lower blood pressure than people who don't own pets. There's even evidence that people at high risk of heart attack because they're hostile have fewer dangerous physical reactions to stress when they have a dog by their side for comfort.

But Rover or Puff can mean even more to your health if you've had a heart attack. A University of Texas-El Paso study shows that pet owners were far more likely to complete a course of cardiac rehabilitation (96%) than those who had no furry friends (77%) were.

Why? A dog or cat might be just the reason you need to get out of bed — and get better. Owning a pet provides a "source of nonjudgmental, unalloyed social support" and unconditional love.

The author, as a widower in retirement in Ann Arbor, Michigan, spent winters in Florida in a house trailer in tropical growth by the side of the Hillsborough River northeast of Tampa. The nearest neighbor offered him the choice from an unexpected litter of six puppies. He chose two females who were the most active and appeared to be the smartest. A few weeks later they wandered away to where some young people were having a cookout. The party had cast off a rather large bone. It was too large for either puppy to retrieve, but he found them paddling down the path home in tandem, each one holding an end of the large bone in her mouth. He had adopted two smart sisters.

Soon after, he shipped them to California by air to a close friend in the Berkeley Hills. There they lived entertaining their master until their deaths 14 years later, within a few months of each other. Their names were Cassie and Polly. Cassie was the smartest, Polly the handsomest. They had frolicked together all their lives and had furnished dear companionship.

Caring for a dog, cat, or other pet is a rare opportunity to be needed and appreciated. On returning home, we always have someone to greet us. A pet's love is without conditions, without limits, without questions. We may never find anything comparable to the loyalty of a pet.

If living where no pets are allowed, a lifelike dog sitting by the master's chair can guard the door, and a soft, furry cat can straddle the back of the couch for the mistress. There is less return of love with stuffed animals, but fewer responsibilities. Still an occasional pat is renewal for the patter.

Chapter Four

MAKING A DIFFERENCE

"The first requisite of a good citizen in this Republic of ours is that he shall be able and willing to pull his weight" — *Theodore Roosevelt*

Introduction

Personal Characteristics for Making a Difference

Dr. Heschel's Guides from the First White House Conference on Aging

The Bible Reduced to Novel Length for Ideas and Inspiration

Forming a Philosophy of Life

Activism Opportunities Abound

Books That Can Make a Difference

INTRODUCTION

In later years it is interesting that increasing the amount of material goods contributes very little to psychological well-being. Happiness and simplicity are separate items and cannot be bought! One difference is that we can volunteer services wanting in society. Reeducation and service projects, whether small or large, never cease as long as we breathe.

We have more time to become watchdogs for clean political campaigns and legislative proposals at all levels, for making an end run around the money chase in political campaigns. A great hope for a better future lies in the emerging independence and force of women as leaders. We can even move to bigger issues, such as global warming, acid rain, water purity, and electing responsible representatives at the local, state, national, and world levels. Push forward with the energy of ages 60 to 120! One immediate approach is to turn off the spinmeisters and talking heads that are proliferating on television, radio, and in newspapers and magazines. We can do our own research.

The growth of grass roots politics and coalition politics offers some fresh air. Sample groups are the League of Women Voters, The Sierra Club, and the Green Party. Health care and child care are examples of issues to take up. Why leave these to the pseudo-expert commentators. Talking head "gasballs" are stealing space from respected analysts. There are now at least six networks instead of three and the number of program channels they are spawning number in the hundreds. One third or more of air time is advertising. Hopefully Ben Bradlee is right, "The ultimate truth will emerge, despite the spinners, despite the cover ups." Close to 79 billion dollars per year is spent for advertising in newspapers, magazines, radio, television, direct mail, yellow pages, and other sources. What a barrage to weed out.

PERSONAL CHARACTERISTICS FOR MAKING A DIFFERENCE

Peak performance comes from ordinary people who accomplish extraordinary things because they recognize a problem and have a sense of mission. To show the power of a single person doing a single act, witness a black woman domestic, Rosa Parks, in Montgomery, Alabama, who sat down in a bus seat and by refusing to move, she made a whole world begin to stand up to the civil rights struggle that led to the resolving of a social sore in American life. There are others in the century just past who through activism made a difference. To mention a few: Saul Alinsky, Hannah Arendt, Daniel Bell, Robert Bellah, Robert Coles, Herbert Gans, Al Gore, Eric Hoffer, Christopher Jencks, Harold Laswell, Seymour Lipset, Gloria Steinem, Studs Terkel, James Q. Wilson. The reader knows many others. There is increasing inequality in financial wealth where it is estimated that 1% of households own close to 50% of household wealth. Similar concentration led to the 1930s Great Depression.

Useful ways to espouse a cause are all around us. Collectively people make a difference. There are neighborhood and telephone networks, voter registrations, resolutions, petitions, hearings, letters to the editor, boycotts, peaceful marches, collecting proxies for greater influence at meetings, action committees in existing organizations, law suits, small claim courts, and political action messages by inexpensive telegrams to state and national representatives.

Some have made a great difference just by writing about a problem.

An American Dilemma by Gunner Myrdal
The Economy of Cities by Jane Jacobs
Cities and the Wealth of Nations by Jane Jacobs
The Other America by Michael Harrington
What to Do with Your Bad Car by Ralph Nader
Who's Poisoning America: Corporate Polluters & Their Victims in the Chemical Age by Ralph Nader

Rachel Carson wrote about saving the living world from the damage done by poison chemicals. In an interview she said people are a part of nature and the war against nature is inevitably a war against people. Before there was an environmental movement, this brave woman had a very brave book, *Silent Spring*, a silent world she was trying to save. Unfortunately, she died early of cancer at age 56.

Among people in history who have made a great difference are Moses, Jesus, Gandhi, and Martin Luther King, Jr. In the one million person march on Washington, D.C. two months before his assassination, King said,

"Everybody can be great because everybody can serve. You don't have to have a college degree to serve; you don't have to make your nouns and verbs agree to serve... You only need a heart full of grace and a soul generated by love."

Now that more people will be living 60 to 120 there is a new segment of society. They have new time in which to make a difference!

To gain perspective, if the current world's population were represented by 100 people, 59 would be Asian, 21 European, 14 Americans (North and South), and 8 African. 70 of the 100 would be nonwhite. Only 30 would be Christian. Fifty per cent of the wealth would be in the hands of 6 of the 100 people. Eighty of the hundred would be living in substandard housing. Only 1 of the 100 would have a college education.

The world is outgrowing the earth's ecosystem and requires cooperation across boundaries that are constantly shrinking. It is already known that sometime in the new century passenger planes will enter upper space with no air resistance flying at 800 miles per hour to almost anywhere in the world in two hours. The world becomes so small that the world's people will need to be joined in new fellowship. The bottom line is that ordinary people accomplish extraordinary things when they recognize they have a sense of mission. Progress comes from learning together, feeling and acting together, leaving no one behind. New insights are needed to live in one world.

Calvin Trilling of The New Yorker alerts readers that with the explosion of television channels, many commentators and columnists may fill space with the absence of expertise and any sufficient knowledge. Notable exceptions are Jim Lehrer, Pamella Wallin, and Brian Lamb. Among the better newspapers to read: from the East are The New York Times and Washington Post; from the Midwest The Cleveland Plain Dealer, The Chicago Tribune, and The St. Louis Post Dispatch; from the South The Atlanta Constitution, and from the West The San Francisco Chronicle and <u>The Los Angeles Times</u>.

Many qualified to vote are failing to vote. Among the 163 democratic nations in the world today, the United States ranks 139th in citizen participation, according to a think tank based in Sweden. In 1998 voter turnout of eligible voters in the U.S. fell to 36%, the lowest per cent in 56 years. Voting by 18 to 24 year olds was even lower at 32%. Americans 65 and over maintained the highest voter turnout of any group, more than 60%. If one wants to get involved, there is power in volunteering. The real concern is the sustainability of the world's environment for a prosperous future. Concerns are about global warming, the global economy, the sustainability of local communities, the promotion of justice, the elimination of poverty, the need to focus on consensus building, the maintaining of wetlands and water quality, recycling and waste management, transportation alternatives, and land and natural resource management. We must be concerned about who is downstream and downwind. The use of sunlight for energy needs rethinking. Even education needs rethinking to create new visions and values.

No one is perfect in making a difference, but we can score ourselves on a ten point scale, ten being high and 1 being low. Then we can start raising our score by talking to friends, writing letters to the editor, city council members, the county board, state officials, one's national Congress person, and even the President.

To multiply one's power, join organizations. The spirit of making a difference is love and working together in common efforts to help one another.

There are numerous ways to get involved. One can make one's own list. Below are some suggestions:

- Lay leader counselor
- Executive service corps
- Sick and handicap visitor
- Activist for world peace
- Political party activist
- Current events leader/member
- AARP activist
- Adult literacy teacher
- Teacher's aide
- Service to the handicapped
- World hunger, poverty & literacy
- Employment finder/counselor
- Historical preservation
- Environmental protection

Skills (over lapping)

- Caring and listening
- Communication
- Optimism
- Vision
- Energy
- Humor
- Tolerance
- Patience
- Creativity
- Consistency
- Mediation
- Collaboration
- Gentleness
- Honesty

The procedure for speeding progress in group discussion is for all to use *Robert's Rules of Order.* The discussion is moved forward by procedures used in this order:

- A main motion on the question to be discussed
- This is amendable or referred to a committee for further information
- A motion to limit debate (requires a 2/3 vote)
- A move to the previous question (requires a 2/3 vote)
- A question of privilege (requires a hand vote of 50+%)
- A move to table the question (requires a hand vote of 50+%)
- A vote by majority

DR. HESCHEL'S GUIDES FROM THE FIRST
WHITE HOUSE CONFERENCE ON AGING

Socrates said wealth does not bring goodness, but goodness brings wealth. Goodness, he said, brings truth and understanding and purification of the soul.

Not all investments in life are made with money and material objects. A contemporary who developed this idea was Rabbi Abraham Joshua Heschel. He emigrated from Poland, escaping death from the Gestapo in Warsaw to the freedom that is America. In the 1960s he held the Henry Emerson Fosdick Chair at Union Theological Seminary in New York.

Dr. Heschel presented a paper to the First White House Conference on Aging in 1961. He called it "To Grow in Wisdom." He felt we all can be full of riches as we grow older -- that each of us is a gold mine. Here are ten of his insights on self-fulfillment:

1. Associate with people who show compassion and understanding for other people — associate with people concerned with events and inner life, not material things. Instead of things, people need goals to strive for.

2. Practice the art of relaxation — through sleep, through sports, through good talk with friends. Keep in training through self-discipline and living a simple life.

3. Find moments of exultation — to stand a little bit above the circumstances of life to get a perspective, a wider horizon.

4. Continue learning — the greatest adventure — full of joy, inspiration and surprise. Learning gives us the gift of freedom and with freedom a person can do anything.

5. Nurture the sense of the unique that is in each person. Of over four and one-half billion faces in this world, no two faces are alike. In each deed we carry out, in each choice we are unique. The potentiality for greatness exists in each individual choice. The meaning of existence and our uniqueness is in facing problems. Heschel would judge a person by how deep are the problems he is concerned with. A person with no problems has nothing.

6. The greatest problem of human existence is to fight against lying; the most important words are honesty and trust. The tragedy of our time is that we do not trust each other.

7. The usefulness of a person is not equivalent to his usefulness to society or his usefulness to other people and their needs. What we are able to bestow on others is usually less and rarely more than a tithe (10%). The usefulness of a person is in being significant and valuable in himself; in one's productivity, one's dreams, one's power to act on problems. Human existence cannot derive its ultimate meaning from society, because society itself is in need of meaning. It is the individual who lends meaning to the human race. It is as individuals that we are beset with desires, fears, and hopes — challenged – endowed with the power of will and a spark of responsibility.

8. Life is a celebration or can be a celebration — a moment of insight, a memory of love, a dream of excellence, a call to worship. There is much entertainment in our life. Instead of participating in spiritual celebration we seek to be amused or entertained. And entertainment is destroying much of our initiative and weakening our imagination. What is really important in life is a celebration – inspiration, song, ritual, prayer, sharing significant moments with friends.

9. Time is life and to kill time is murder. Most of us labor for the things of space -- possessions. But things are forgeries of happiness, they are a threat to our very lives. Time is a person's most important frontier; the advance region of significant being, a region where a person's true freedom lies. Space divides us, time unites us. We wage wars over things of space; the treasures of time lie open to every person.

10. Every moment is an opportunity for greatness. People have been anxious to save money for later years -- they should also be anxious to prepare a spiritual income of wisdom, maturity, and tranquility. People need a vision, not only recreation. People need a dream, not only a memory.

By applying Heschel's ten insights everyone can profit and contribute to individual self-fulfillment and to the well-being of all. The American dream is one big tent where no one should be in the margins. We must leave no one behind as we value diversity. Women and people of other hues are all included as productive citizens in creating a stronger society.

THE BIBLE REDUCED TO NOVEL LENGTH
FOR IDEAS AND INSPRIATION

The Bible is probably the most powerful book that has ever been produced, shaping who and what we are in profound ways. To a large degree cultural understandings have been drawn from Biblical language.

The message of love that is central to the text of the Bible has inspired men like Francis of Assisi to love and care for animals, women like Clara Barton to love and care for the wounded in the Civil War, women like Dorothy Day to love and care for the down-trodden in New York City, men like Albert Schweitzer to love and care for the forgotten in Africa.

The Ten Commandments, the numerous injunctions scattered throughout the Jewish and Christian texts to be just, the images of a messianic age found in the Prophets have all had a powerful effect in inspiring people to improve themselves and to work for a better society.

The Bible can be summarized by omitting the mass of historical data in the King James Version (Protestant) or the Rheims Duiay Version (Catholic). What follows is Smith and Goodspeed's Version reduced by outline to novel length.

Selected Readings from the Old Testament:

From the five books in the Pentateuch, the beginning, and Moses' work and law.

The story of Cain; help each other; we are our brothers' keeper
— GENESIS: 4:2-12

The story of Noah: we cannot trample on the sacred or get

swept away — GENESIS: 6,7,8

The story of Joseph: get busy where we are
— GENESIS: 39:21-23

Omit the 12 Historical Books on the rise and fall of the Hebrew nation, the people selected for the coming of Jesus. Omit the 5 Poetical Books, the literature of the Hebrew nation's Golden Age.

A drama on the conquest of human suffering — JOB (all)

Feelings in poetry praising God and the good man — Selected
PSALMS:1, 8, 15, 18, 19, 23, 24, 34, 37, 62, 65, 82, 84,90, 91,96,
97, 100, 103, 104, 108 (16-20), 111, 112, 116, 121, 127, 128,
133, 138, 139 (1-12), 141, 144 (12-15), 145, 146, 147, & 148.

The wise sayings of Solomon — PROVERBS: 1-31

Maxims for the cultivation of wisdom
— ECCLESIASTES: 1-12

The glory of wedded love — SONG OF SOLOMON: 1-13

Omit the 17 Prophetical Books: The Hebrew nation's Dark Days and God's struggle with idolatry.

Selected Readings from the New Testament

These 27 books on Christianity repeat the idea of God to love your neighbor and recognize men's worth and dignity, as brought to the world by Jesus and his Apostles. The coming, the life, and teachings of Jesus are found in the four Gospels: Matthew, Mark, Luke, and John.

The six great teachings of Jesus — MATTHEW

The Sermon on the Mount: Verses 5, 6, & 7

Directions to the Apostles: give self and fear nothing:
Verse 10

On the seashore: see, hear, and understand, and the
    lessons will yield many fold: Verse 13
Answering the Disciples: on forgiveness: Verse 18
To the crowds on the virtues: Verse 23
On the Mount of Olives; brotherly love: Verses 24 & 25
On money as master — LUKE: 16
On using one's resources — LUKE: 19
What is God? — JOHN: 14
Paul's labor for the idea that Christianity is not just for Jews
but for all nations — ACTS (all)
The Letters: 21 books of Paul interpreting Christianity
    Paul's teachings — ROMANS: 12, 13, 14, & 15
    On the care of the body and human endowments —
        I CORINTHIANS: 5,(9-13), 6(9-20), 12, & 13
    On confidence — II CORINTHIANS: 3(12-18), 4, 5, & 6
    On living by the spirit — GALATIANS: 5(13-20),6(1-10)
    On the worthwhile life — EPHESIANS: 3,4,5,6
    On life with Christ — COLOSSIANS: 3
    On self-dependence — I THESSALONIANS: 4(1-12)
    Love of money as the root of all evils — I TIMOTHY: 1-6
    Faith — II TIMOTHY: 1-4
    Devotion to doing good — TITUS: 1-3
    On faith and discipline — HEBREWS: 11,12,13
    On understanding the good — JAMES: 1-5
    On married life and love for one another — I PETER: 3,4
    On understanding Jesus — II PETER: 1
    On brotherly love — I JOHN: 3,4,5

Brotherly love will triumph through long struggles, failures, partial victories, and compromise — REVELATION: (all)

Both the Old and New Testaments, whether read partially or entirely, offer guidance and inspiration for all generations.

LOCKING IN A PHILOSOPHY OF LIFE

I . My goals are _____

_____

_____

2. I spend my time _____

_____

_____

3. I would like to learn _____

_____

_____

4. Two activities in which I have felt most alive and vibrant as a
person are _____

_____

_____

5. If I could have three wishes for enriching life, they would be

_____

_____

_____

_____

6. Happiness is _____

_____

_____

_____

7. Other _____

_____

_____

_____

_____

ACTIVISM OPPORTUNITIES ABOUND

Unbridled growth has brought unbridled environmental damage. A United Nations study finds only 20% of the world's population accounts for 86% of private consumption and unlimited growth. Goods for the market do not reconstitute themselves after having been used. Ultimately they are transposed into waste products. Burning gas in cars releases carbon dioxide; manufacture of pesticides often produces toxic waste. The seminal book The *Limits to Growth* suggests a longer view might well be to invest in mass transit.

Conservation organizations are now working just to save wilderness, water, and air quality, but also agricultural land, family farms and ranches, local food markets, fine old buildings, and scenic roads. There is hardly a farm, locally owned store, shop, restaurant, or small business anywhere that is not struggling to save itself. Are people being forgotten? Are public lands being protected from rape and pillage? Healthy ecosystems are essential parts of citizens' needs for clean air, safe usable land, and an overall safe environment.

Rotary, Kiwanis, Optimists, and numerous other community service organizations have it right. Action programs offer opportunity for making a difference for the total society. A starter list includes the following:

Local service programs for development
Habitat for Humanity — swinging a hammer or a paint brush
Teaching English to immigrants
Elderhostel service programs
Teaching and camping for special children
Volunteer curators

Conservation of natural resources
Community development
Housing shelters
Recycling of paper, cardboard, etc.
Bring a dog or cat to visit the elderly
Needed recreation programs
Community park beautification
Salvation Army projects, such as clothing distribution
Removing paints, solvents, and toxins
Helping with transportation, such as getting out the vote
Removing graffiti
Food banks

Can spiritual vigor expand to permit living in one world? Designed political strategies facilitate improvements for the benefit of everyone. As an example, in North Carolina Barnardsville, along with nearby Asheville, adopted a forest that is home to fifty species of rare endangered plants and animals. It is the Pisgah National Forest of 14,000 acres, one of the largest repositories of unprotected forest in the United States. The Southern Appalachians have some of the greatest biodiversity in a temperate region anyplace in the world. This diversity translates into a beauty that is overwhelming, like a symphony. And there are redwoods in California and mid-America forests that need similar protection.

In contrast over-consumption increases. At Neiman Marcus in New York City there is an 18 month waiting list for $10,000 handbags. Wrist watches at over $2,000 are the fastest selling item. The public needs knowledge of what is happening to resources.

Every year that goes by without controls pushes the limits of irreplaceable resources.

Long range planning can be rewarding. The Hudson River, like many American streams, was once given up as dead. Today it abounds with life. People now swim in it, unthinkable 30 years ago. At home we can stop dumping toxic substances in the garbage or down the drain. Without reading labels, citizens throw batteries of all kinds into the garbage. In the United States alone there is the problem of cleaning up nearly 50 years of toxic substances in our soils and waters.

Larger and larger chain outlets are crowding out independent businesses, creating dreary architectural malls along previous farmland along more freeways to disperse the population. Vital neighborhoods and city and town businesses are being sapped of their life blood due to urban sprawl. When is enough enough?

Aldo Leopold asks in *A Sand Country Almanac,* "has America become so obsessed with its individual economic health as to have lost the capacity to be healthy?" The billions spent on arms and conflict can be resolved by universal peace to contribute to the common good of humankind! Perhaps women will lead the way. They now outnumber men enrolled in college. They are more caring, and they are living longer. Early in the new century there will be a woman President of the United States!

Education is an opportunity available over the entire life span. Knowledge is available as never before and is free for the taking. In lifelong learning there is salvation. Aging confers freedom never before enjoyed. Active elders are cherished and loved for their experiences and wisdom. The late years can be the happiest of life, not enjoyed by earlier generations. Added is opportunity for making a difference, keeping an eye on the prize!

The best way to end this chapter on making a difference is with models of conflict resolution from the century just passed.

- Martin Luther King, Jr. for nonviolence and brotherhood
- Margaret Fuller and Joanne Williams for world peace
- Helen Keller for optimism and faith
- Mohandas Gandhi for passive resistance and independence
- Jane Addams and Dorothy Day for housing and women's rights
- Pete Seeger for saving the environment
- E.F. Schumacher for small being beautiful
- Henry David Thoreau for renewal from nature
- Mother Teresa for doing small things with love
- Mary (Mother) Jones for creative organizing
- Dalai Lama for peace for the whole world
- Carl Sagan for space vision

We predict that diseases such as heart disease, cancer, Alzheimer's disease, and arthritis will be controlled; and that society can insure to all adequate food, shelter, continued education, and the absence of wars and violence. We can have a person-oriented society, producing a flowering of the spirit that becomes a journey toward wholeness for everyone.

The idea of living beyond the century mark of 100 to 120 years is appealing. About 90% of centenarians are women. We need to discover why. It should be as possible to add quality in aging for men as it is for women. Some aches, pains, and memory lapses need not mean a decline in the ability to enjoy life. Actually, individual happiness increases in late maturity with the satisfactions that come from a life well lived. Years of experience over younger counterparts create positive emotions and mental toughness. Having reached the top of the mountain, supported by spiritual beliefs, the older person can become a miracle in the making with many new experiences yet to explore!

FINALLY, SOME BOOKS THAT CAN MAKE A DIFFERENCE IN OUR ASPIRATIONS AND ACCOMPLISHMENTS:

The Age of Reason	Thomas Paine
The Americanization of Edward Bok	Edward Bok
The American Scholar	Ralph W. Emerson
The Art of Happiness	The Dalai Lama
The Art of Loving	Erich Fromm
Autobiography of Lincoln Steffens	Lincoln Steffens
Autobiography of Malcolm X	Malcolm X
The Best and the Brightest	David Halbertstam
Cry, the Beloved Country	Alan Paton
The Culture of Cities	Lewis Mumford
Edison, a Biography	Matthew Josephson
The Human Mind	Karl Menninger
Invisible Man	Ralph Ellison
Das Kapital	Karl Marx
Leaves of Grass	Walt Whitman
Letters from a Father to His Daughter	Jawaharlal Nehru
Life and Times of Frederick Douglass	Frederick Douglass
Living My Life	Emma Goldman
Living the Good Life	Scott & Helen Nearing
Madame Curie	Eve Curie
Main Currents in American Thought	Vernon Parrington
Markings	Dag Hammarskjold
New Science of Politics	Eric Voegelin
Our Plundered Planet	Fairfield Osborn
Peace of Mind	Joshua Liebman
Preface to Morals	Walter Lippmann
The School of Work	Mao Tse-Tung
Self-Renewal	John Gardner
The True Believer	Eric Hoffer
Working It Out	Sara Ruddick & Pamela Daniels

DAILY REMINDERS FOR LIVING IT UP TO REACH 100+

Vitality

- Mastering nutrition and access to health care
- Morning exercises and indoor/outdoor walks
- Visiting with friends and discovering new ones
- Less driving and more public transport

Creativity

- Finding the best news, magazines, and books
- Affiliating with active aging groups
- Doing independent research
- Gardening indoors and out

Fun Function

- Sampling books, stories, and films
- Sitting to commune with nature
- Being a sports, arts, and music fan
- Making photo and favorite cut-out scrapbooks

Making a Difference

- Keeping productive in home and community activities
- Continuing spiritual development
- Being in giving and support networks
- Keeping politically active

USEFUL RELATED SOURCES

Abbey, Edward	*A Voice Cryng in the Wilderness,* 1998
Abramovitch, Janet	*Taking a Stand: the World's Forests,* 1998
Adams, E. M.	*A Society Fit for Human Beings,* 1997
Albom, Mitch	*Tuesdays with Morrie,* 1997
Allen, John G.	*A Guide to Self-Understanding,* 1995
Allen, Lacy	*The Inviting Garden,* 1998
Andrews, Molly	*Lifetime of Commitments,* 1991
Argyle, Michael	*The Psychology of Happiness,* 1987
Atchley, R. C.	*Social Forces in Aging,* 1991
	Backpacker -- Magazine of Wilderness Travel
Baugman, James	*The Republic of Mass Culture,* 1997
Benson, Herbert	*The Relaxation Response,* 1976
Binstock, Robert H.	*The Future of Long-Term Care,* 1996
Birren, James	*Building Autobiography, Older Adults,* 1996
Bortz, Walter	*Dare to Be 100,* 1995
Borysenko, Joan	*Minding the Body, Minding the Mind,* 1988
Boyte, Harry	*Building America,* 1996
Brown, Lester	*State of the World,* 1998
Buck, Susan	*The Global Commons,* 1998
Butler, Robert	*Aging and Mental Health: Positive Approaches,* 1977
Butler, Robert	*Being Old in America,* 1985
Cameron, Donald	*The Living Beach,* 1997

Campbell, Joseph	*The Hero with a Thousand Faces,* 1968
Carter, Jimmy	*Virtues of Aging,* 1998
Cartledge, Bryan	*Health and Environment,* 1994
Cecil, Andrew	*Moral Values, the Challenges of the 21st Century,* 1996
Cecil, Andrew	*Chase's Annual Events,* 2000
Chopra, Deepak	*Healing the Heart,* 1998
Coleman, Linda	*Women's Life Writing,* 1997
Coles, Robert	*Old Ones on Their Own,* 1994
Condeluci, A.	*Beyond Difference,* 1996
Cousins, Norman	*Anatomy of an Illness,* 1979
Cronkite, Walter	*50 Forever,* 1998
Crose, Royda	*Why Women Live Longer Than Men,* 1997
Csikszenti, Mihalyi	*The Creative Spirit,* 1992
Csikszenti, Mihalyi	The Psychology of Engagement, 1997
<u>Daedalus</u>	"The Liberation of the Environment" Summer 1996
de Bono, Edward	*Creativity Step by Step,* 1970
Denby, David	*Great Books,* 1996
Dower, Roger	*Frontiers of Sustainability,* 1997
Downs, Hugh	*Fifty and Forever,* 1994
Dychtwald, Ken	*Age Wave, The Challenges and Opportunities of Aging,* 1998
Dyson, Kenneth	*Culture First, Standards in the Media Age,* 1996
Eckholm, Erik	*The Picture of Health,* 1997
Ehrenfeld, David	*Beginning Again, The New Millennium,* 1993
Elliott, David	*Energy, Society, and Environment,* 1997

Elliott, Michael	*The Day Before Yesterday*, 1996
Fierstein, Roger	*Leading on the Creative Edge*, 1996
Folger, Janet	*Improving Your Memory*, 1976
Fossel, Michael	*Reversing Human Aging*, 1996
Frantzich & Sullivan	*The C-Span Revolution*, 1996
Friedan, Betty	*The Fountains of Age*, 1993
Friedan, Betty	*Beyond Gender*, 1997
Goleman, Daniel	*Emotional Intelligence*, 1995
Goleman, David	*The Creative Spirit*, 1992
Gordon, James	*Manifesto for a New Medicine*, 1996
Green, Bob	*Make the Connection: 10 Steps to a Better Body*, 1996
Greenbach Doris	*Coming into the End Zone*, 1991
Hampson, Fen, ed.	*People, Land, and Community*, 1997
Hannon, Hildegard, ed.	*Earthly Goods, Environmental Change*, 1996
Headstrom, Richard	*Adventures with a Hand Lens*, 1976
Hempell, Lamont	*Environmental Governance*, 1996
Herzog, Regula	*Health and Economic Status of Older Women*, 1989
Hobson, J.A.	*The Social Problem*, 1996
Hufford, Mary	*The Great Generation, Memory, Mastery, Legacy*, 1987
Imbrocio, David	*Reconstructing City Politics*, 1997
Isard, Walter	*Commonalities in Art, Science, Religion*, 1996
Jason, Leonard	*Community Building*, 1997
Jarmieson, Lynn	*Intimacy: Personal Relationship in Modern Societies*, 1998

Jebens, Harley	*100 Jobs in Social Change*, 1996
Johns Hopkins- White Papers	*Memory*, 1998 *Arthritis, Low Back Pain,* 1998
Johnson, Allen	*The Forest and the Trees, Sociology as Life,* 1997
Kari, Nancy and Boyle, Harry	*Building America*, 1997
Kay, Jay Holtz	*Asphalt Nation*, 1997
Khalsa, D.S. and Staub, C.	*Brain Longevity*, 1997
Khgchaturian, Z.S.	*Alzheimer's Disease, Diagnosis, Treatment, Care,* 1997
Kimball, Richard	*The Winds of Creativity*, 1996
Liberman, Morton	*Doors Close, Doors Open*, 1996
Lowenfeld, Victor	*Creativity and Mental Growth*, 1982
Ludington, Ailsen	*Dynamic Living*, 1995
McGowin, Diana	*Living in the Labyrinth, Alzheimer's,* 1993
Mace, Nancy and Rabins, Peter	*The 36-Hour Day*, 1991
Maddox, George, ed.	*Encyclopedia of Aging*, 1995
May, Rollo	*The Courage to Create*, 1976
MIT Press	*Critical Conditions, Human Health*, 1996
Moeler, David	*Environmental Health*, 1992
Moore, A.D.	*Invention, Discovery, and Creativity*, 1969
Moore, Thomas	*The Re-Enchantment of Everyday Life*, 1996
Mullen, Patrick	*Listening to Old Voices*, 1992
National Research Council	*Environmentally Significant Consumption,* 1997

New York Times
Magazine   "God Decentralized", December 7, 1997

Peck, M. Scott   *The Road Less Traveled*, 1985

Peterson, Peter   *Will America Grow Up Before Growing Old*, 1996

Rhoads, Robert   *Community Service: Exploration of the Caring Self*, 1997

Restag, Richard   *The Longevity Strategy*, 1998

Rippe, James   *Fit Over Forty*, 1996

Rowe, John and
Kahn, Robert   *Successful Aging*, 1998

Sampson, A. & S.   *The Oxford Book of Ages*, 1985

Scharma, S. Ram   *Women and Education*, 1995

Scheeze, Don   *Nature Writing*, 1996

Schumacker, E.F.   *Small is Beautiful*, 1975

Sears, Barry   *The Anti-Aging Zone*, 1999

Sheehy, Gail   *Understanding Men's Passages*, 1999

Shepard, Roy   *The Health Consequences of Modernization*, 1996

Short, John R.   *New Worlds, New Geographies*, 1998

Shuldiner, David   *Folklore, Culture, and Aging*, 1997

Siegel, Bernie   *Love, Medicine, and Miracles*, 1986

Simonton, Carl   *Getting Well Again*, 1978

Smith, J. M. &
Goodspeed, E. J.   *The Bible, (* A Modern Translation*)*, 1935

Suzman, Richard   *The Oldest Old*, 1995

Teske, Nathan   *Political Activists in America*, 1997

Theodosakis, Jason   *Maximizing the Arthritis Cure*, 1998

Torrance, E. Paul   *Creativity*, 1969

Vaugn, Susan	*Viagra, A Guide to Potency*, 1998
Wakefield, Dan	*Creating from Spirit,* 1996
Warshofsky, Fred	*Stealing Time: The New Science of Aging,* 1999
Weaver, Frances	*I'm as Old as I Used to Be*, 1997
Webster, Donovan	*Aftermath*, 1996
Weis, Rich	"Aging – New Answers" National Geographic, November 1, 1997
Weis, Thomas & Collins, Cindy	*Humanitarian Challenges*, 1996
Werthman, Paul	*Religion and Contemporary Liberalism*,1997
White, Donald	*Postmodern Ecology*, 1998
Wimberley, Anne	*Honoring African-American Elders*, 1997
Wolfe, Alan	*Marginalized in the Middle*, 1996
Wolfe, Alan	*One Nation After All*, 1998
Wolff, Edward	*Top Heavy*, 1996
Zaret, Barry	*Yale School of Medicine Health Book*, 1992
Zibergeld, Bernie	*The Truth about Sex & Pleasure*, 1992

ABOUT THE AUTHOR

Bob Plummer, at age 85, is as craggy as the farm in southern Indiana's limestone region where he was born. He earned degrees from Wabash College (A.B.), Indiana University (Ed.D.), and the University of Michigan (MPH). His first career was as an accountant at General Electric in Schenectady. Changing careers, he became a high school teacher in Bedford, Crawfordsville, and Ft. Wayne in Indiana. Later he became a college professor at Purdue and Northwestern Universities, a dean at the University of Michigan-Flint, and President of Lake Michigan College.

He served as a senior deck watch officer on the U.S.S. Raleigh (CL 7) in the Pacific during World War II.

In retirement, his speaker's bureau offers *Carl Sandburg Live* to audiences in the Midwest and South with poetry, folktales, and excerpts from Sandburg's six volumes on Abraham Lincoln. The Plummers reside at Glacier Hills in Ann Arbor, Michigan.

Previous publications:
The Wasbash, 1936, Journal Review Press, Crawfordsville,
    Indiana
Needs of 9th Grade Students, 1951, Indiana University, Bloomington,
    Indiana
The Two Year College, 1965, Prentice-Hall, Englewood Cliffs,
    New Jersey
College, Careers, and You, 1971, Science Research Associates, IBM,
    Chicago, Illinois

Plummer spent the first half of his mature life teaching and publishing for America's youth. In late life he researches and writes for this same group as they become the new elderly.